Manifestation: Make the Law of Attraction Work for You.

Written By

Kanav Sachdev

My Authors Hub

A unit of FanatiXx® Publication

AM/56, Basanti Colony, Rourkela 769012, Odisha

ISO 9001:2015 Certified

© Copyright, 2023 Kanav Sachdev

By: Kanav Sachdev

ISBN: 978-93-6244-697-8

Book: Manifestation : Make the law of attraction work for you
Price: INR 1099/-
Printing By: BooksClub.in

The opinions/ contents expressed in this book are the sole of the author and do not represent the opinions/ stands/ thoughts of FanatiXx® or any of its associates and affiliations.

Acknowledgement

In the journey of bringing "Manifestation: Make the Law of Attraction Work for You" to life, I've been blessed with the support, inspiration, and guidance of remarkable individuals. This book is not just a solitary effort; it's a collaborative manifestation of shared wisdom and collective energy.

First and foremost, I express my deepest gratitude to the Universe, the boundless source of inspiration and creativity. Your energies have guided every word and intention in this book.

To my family, whose unwavering support has been my anchor. Thank you for understanding the late nights, the scattered notebooks, and the endless pursuit of a vision. Your love is my greatest manifestation.

To my friends, for being the sounding board for crazy ideas and the champions of dreams. Your encouragement has been the wind beneath my wings.

To my editor, your keen eye and constructive feedback transformed this manuscript. Your dedication to polishing every word is evident on every page.

Gratitude to the incredible team at Epiphany Publishing, whose passion for literature and commitment to excellence turned this manuscript into a beautiful reality.

To the vibrant community on social media, thank you for sharing your stories, insights, and manifestations. Your energy reverberates through these pages.

Finally, to the readers. Thank you for embarking on this journey with me. May "Manifestation" be a catalyst for positive transformation in your life.

This book is a manifestation of collective energy, love, and shared dreams. May its ripples of positivity extend far and wide.

With heartfelt gratitude,

Kanav Sachdev
FEB 2024.

Disclaimer

This book has been published with all reasonable efforts taken to make the material error free after the consent of the author. No part of this book shall be used, reproduced in any manner whatsoever without written permission from the author, except in the case of brief quotations embodied in critical articles and reviews.

Foreword
Unleashing the Power Within

Welcome to a journey that transcends the boundaries of ordinary existence. As I stand at the threshold of introducing you to "Manifestation: Make the Law of Attraction Work for You," I am filled with a profound sense of anticipation. This book is not just a collection of words on paper; it is a guide to unlocking the extraordinary potential nestled within each of us.

In a world pulsating with constant motion, it is easy to forget the innate power we possess—the ability to shape our reality through the deliberate orchestration of our thoughts, beliefs, and intentions. "Manifestation" is not a mere exploration of this power; it is an invitation to wield it consciously, purposefully, and with unwavering intent.

This journey began not as a quest for esoteric knowledge, but as a personal odyssey. As I navigated the ebb and flow of life, I stumbled upon the transformative principles that underlie the art of manifestation. The insights gained from moments of triumph and the lessons learned in the crucible of challenge form the foundation of the wisdom I share within these pages.

As you embark on this expedition, be prepared to encounter not just theories but practical tools, not just words but a roadmap for personal evolution. Each chapter is a gateway, a portal into the realms of self-discovery, positive transformation, and the boundless potential that resides within you.

"Manifestation: Make the Law of Attraction Work for You" is not a destination; it is a guide for crafting a journey—a journey towards a life of purpose, abundance, and joy. Whether you are drawn to manifesting financial prosperity, cultivating love and relationships, nurturing health and well-being, or achieving success in your career, the principles unveiled here are universal and adaptable.

Consider this book not as a dictation of truths but as an invitation to explore, question, and experiment. The pages that follow are an offering, a sharing of insights, techniques, and a reservoir of inspiration. Your engagement and willingness to apply what you discover will be the catalyst for the magic that unfolds in your life.

May "Manifestation: Make the Law of Attraction Work for You" be a compass on your path, guiding you through the realms of your own potential. Embrace the power within, for as you do, you'll discover that the life you envision is not a distant dream but a reality waiting to be manifested.

With anticipation and gratitude,
Kanav Sachdev

Author, "Manifestation: Make the Law of Attraction Work for You"

Preface: A Prelude to Possibility

In the quiet moments of reflection that precede the written word, I find myself compelled to share the genesis of "Manifestation: Make the Law of Attraction Work for You." This book is not a proclamation of certainties; rather, it is a conversation, a dialogue between the reader and the endless possibilities that lie within.

As I embarked on this writing journey, I was drawn not only by the magnetic pull of the Law of Attraction but by a deeper curiosity about the human capacity to shape reality. The unfolding pages are a result of years spent exploring the intricacies of manifestation, guided not only by the wisdom of sages and scholars but by the crucible of personal experience.

Within these words, you won't find a rigid doctrine but an invitation to traverse the realms of your own potential. The techniques and insights shared are not mandates but tools, waiting to be wielded by you, the architect of your destiny.

"Manifestation" is not a promise of an effortless journey, for life's tapestry is woven with challenges and triumphs alike. It is an acknowledgment that each thought, every intention, carries the weight of creation. As we delve into the intricacies of making the Law of Attraction work for us, remember that this is not a one-size-fits-all manual but a guidebook for self-discovery.

The real magic of manifestation lies not in the grandeur of external events but in the subtle transformation within. This book is a mirror reflecting the incredible power you hold—the power to sculpt your reality, to manifest a life that resonates with your deepest desires.

As you turn the pages, consider them not as a lecture but as a conversation with a fellow traveler on the path of self-discovery. Feel free to question, to adapt, to make these principles your own. The beauty of manifestation is its adaptability to the unique contours of your journey.

May "Manifestation: Make the Law of Attraction Work for You" be more than a book; may it be a companion on your quest for understanding, growth, and the realization of your dreams.

With anticipation and gratitude,

Kanav Sachdev

Author, "Manifestation: Make the Law of Attraction Work for You

<u>Dedication</u>

This book is dedicated to My Grandparents and My Kids
Late Sh. K L Sachdeva
Late Smt Prakash Devi Sachdeva
Sh RP Grover
Smt Sudershan Grover
Master Yunay Sachdeva
Ms. Kyra Sachdeva
And

"Dedicated to those who believe in the magic of intentional living and the power we hold within to shape our destinies."

वक्रतुण्ड महाकाय सूर्यकोटि समप्रभ ।
निर्विघ्नं कुरु मे देव सर्वकार्येषु सर्वदा ॥

Vakra-Tunndda Maha-Kaaya Suurya-Kotti Samaprabha |
Nirvighnam Kuru Me Deva Sarva-Kaaryessu Sarvadaa ||

Introduction

Have you ever felt stuck and unfulfilled in your life, unsure of how to break free from the limitations holding you back? If so, you're not alone. Many people struggle with the lack of knowledge and understanding about the power of manifestation. But what if I told you that you have the ability to manifest your desires and transform your life? This book, "Manifestation: Make the Law of Attraction Work for you " is here to guide you on the journey to unlocking your full potential.

Understanding the law of attraction is key to harnessing the power of manifestation. Our thoughts and beliefs shape our reality and attract experiences and circumstances into our lives. By gaining a deeper understanding of this universal law, you can consciously create the life you desire. This book will provide you with the knowledge and tools you need to tap into the power of manifestation and manifest your desires.

What sets this guide apart from others on manifestation is its comprehensive and practical approach. With step-by-step techniques, worksheets, and activities, you will have a clear roadmap to follow. By diligently practicing the principles and exercises in this book, you will be able to manifest your desires and create a life of abundance and fulfillment.

The book Starts off by exploring the fundamentals of manifestation. You will learn what manifestation is and how it works, the power of thoughts and beliefs, the role of intention, and the connection between manifestation and energy. This sets the foundation for successful manifestation.

Moving forward the book focuses on preparing yourself for manifestation. You will discover how to cultivate a positive mindset, clear limiting beliefs, create a vision for your life, and set achievable goals. By aligning your thoughts and actions with your desired manifestations, you will be ready to manifest with intention.

Techniques for manifestation are explored and discussed at length. Visualization, affirmations, meditation, gratitude, journaling, and creative expression are powerful tools that will help you harness the power of your thoughts and emotions to manifest your desires.

Further, the book delves deeper into practical tools that enhance manifestation. Creating a vision board, using manifestation rituals and ceremonies, harnessing the power of crystals and gemstones, and incorporating essential oils and aromatherapy will amplify your manifestation process.

Challenges are inevitable in all walks of life and there will be challenges on your manifestation journey as well, which is why the book addresses common obstacles. You will learn how to deal with doubt and skepticism, manage impatience and frustration, navigate setbacks and obstacles, and maintain a positive mindset during challenging times. the book provides strategies to overcome any roadblocks you may encounter.

Manifestation isn't just about achieving material wealth; it encompasses all areas of life. The book further explores manifestation in different areas, including abundance and financial prosperity, love and relationships, health and well-being, and success and career growth. The techniques and tools discussed in previous chapters can be applied to these specific areas.

In the final section, we focus on putting manifestation into action. You will learn how to create a personalized manifestation plan, establish daily practices to stay on track, cultivate patience and trust in the process, and celebrate and acknowledge manifestations. This section will help you integrate manifestation into your daily life.

In conclusion, the power of manifestation has the potential to transform your life in ways you never thought possible. By embracing your desires and goals and following the principles and exercises in this book, you can tap into the limitless potential of your thoughts and intentions. Get ready to manifest the life you truly desire.

Table of contents

Chapter 1: The Power of Manifestation

Understanding the Law of Attraction

The concept of the law of attraction has gained significant popularity in recent years as more and more people strive to understand its power in manifestation. This fascinating idea centers around the belief that our thoughts and beliefs possess the ability to shape our reality. In simpler terms, what we think and believe will attract corresponding experiences into our lives. This understanding is absolutely crucial for anyone seeking to harness the power of manifestation and create a life they genuinely desire. At its core, the law of attraction asserts that like attracts like. Our thoughts and beliefs act as energetic magnets, drawing in similar experiences, people, and opportunities. By intentionally focusing on positive thoughts and beliefs, we can align ourselves with positive outcomes. This is because our thoughts and beliefs exert a profound influence on our experiences. By consistently cultivating thoughts and beliefs that good things will happen, we increase the likelihood of attracting positive outcomes. The impact of our thoughts and beliefs on our reality cannot be overstated. The power of positive thinking is undeniable. When we concentrate our thoughts and energy on what we want to manifest, we effectively communicate our desires to the universe. This communication is then reflected back to us in the form of experiences, people, and opportunities that enter our lives. However, it is important to acknowledge the existence of limiting beliefs that can hinder our manifestations. These deeply ingrained beliefs hold us back from achieving our desires. By identifying and addressing these limiting beliefs, we can remove the barriers to our manifestations.

The connection between our thoughts and emotions is a critical aspect to understanding the law of attraction. Our thoughts have the capacity to trigger certain emotions, and vice versa. For instance, if we consistently entertain positive thoughts, we will typically experience positive emotions such as joy and gratitude. Conversely, negative thoughts can lead to negative emotions like fear and anxiety. Being cognizant of our thoughts and emotions is key to better understanding and harnessing the law of attraction. When we are mindful of our thoughts and emotions, we can consciously choose to shift our focus towards the positive ones, thereby attracting positive manifestations into our lives. Manifestations are the specific experiences, people, or opportunities that we draw into our lives through the law of attraction. Our thoughts and beliefs act as magnets, attracting these manifestations. For instance, if we firmly believe that we deserve a loving relationship, we are more likely to attract a loving partner into our lives. Similarly, by holding onto thoughts and beliefs of financial abundance, we increase the likelihood of attracting financial opportunities and success. The possibilities for manifestations are truly limitless, only constrained by our own beliefs and intentions. Visualization and affirmation are powerful tools when practicing the law of attraction. By visualizing our desired outcomes and affirming them with conviction, we can establish a clear and focused intention. Visualization allows us to vividly imagine what we want to manifest, engaging all our senses in the process. Affirmations are positive statements that reinforce our desires and beliefs. By consistently visualizing and affirming, we align ourselves with the energy of our desires and enhance the likelihood of manifesting them. It is crucial to remain consistent and steadfast in our visualization and affirmation practices, while truly believing in the power of these techniques. While the law of attraction is an influential tool for manifestation, it is important to acknowledge that it may not always work in isolation.

External factors can influence our reality regardless of our thoughts and beliefs. For instance, unexpected events or circumstances may arise that are beyond our control. In such cases, it is important to remember that taking action is just as crucial as focusing on positive thoughts and beliefs. By taking action towards our goals and desires, we actively contribute to creating the reality we desire. Additionally, it is essential to consider the role of privilege and systemic barriers in the law of attraction. Society's structures and inequalities can impact an individual's ability to manifest their desires. Factors such as socioeconomic status, race, and gender can create systemic barriers that limit opportunities for manifestation. Therefore, it is crucial to acknowledge and address these systemic inequalities alongside the law of attraction. By advocating for social change and working towards dismantling these barriers, we can create a more equitable environment for manifestation. Furthermore, one's current circumstances and mindset can affect their ability to manifest desired outcomes. If someone is facing significant challenges or has a negative mindset, it may be more difficult for them to manifest their desires. In these cases, it is important to address underlying issues and engage in personal growth alongside the practice of the law of attraction. By actively working on personal development, we can remove the barriers that hinder our manifestations and create a strong foundation for success. Luck and chance are also factors that can impact our manifestations. Life is inherently unpredictable, and random events or chance occurrences can shape our reality. It is important to acknowledge and accept the unpredictable nature of life while practicing the law of attraction. This does not mean that manifestation is futile, but rather that we must embrace the uncertainty and adapt our approach. By maintaining an open mindset and being flexible in our manifestations, we can navigate the unpredictable nature of life and still create the reality we desire. In conclusion, understanding the law of attraction is a powerful tool for manifestation. By consciously focusing on positive thoughts and beliefs, visualizing and affirming our desires, and taking action towards our goals, we can attract the experiences, people, and opportunities that align with our desires. However, it is important to consider external factors, address systemic inequalities, and engage in personal growth alongside the practice of the law of attraction. By doing so, we create a holistic approach to manifestation that encompasses both internal and external factors.

How This Guide Will Transform Your Life

In this subchapter, I aim to provide a brief introduction and set the context for the transformative power of manifestation. My purpose is to explain how the techniques and practices shared in the following chapters can lead to life-changing experiences. It is crucial to recognize the importance of harnessing the power of thoughts and manifesting our desires in order to create the reality we truly desire.

Defining Terms:

To ensure a clear understanding, let me define key terms that will be frequently used throughout this book. "Transformative power" refers to the ability to bring about significant and positive changes in one's life. "Techniques" and "practices" encompass specific methods and approaches that can be employed to cultivate personal growth and transformation. "Harnessing thoughts" involves the deliberate act of directing our thinking towards desired outcomes, while "manifesting desires" refers to the process of bringing these desired outcomes into reality.

These terms hold great significance in the context of personal growth and transformation. By understanding and actively engaging with them, we can unlock our full potential and create the life we envision.

Objectives and Scope:

In this subchapter, my goal is to highlight the transformative power of this book and discuss how the techniques and practices shared can lead to personal transformation. I will cover a range of topics, including mindset shifts, visualization exercises, and goal-setting strategies. By delving into these areas, readers will gain valuable insights and actionable steps towards their own transformational journey.

Methodology and Approach:

To support the claims made in this subchapter, I draw upon a variety of methods and approaches. These include referencing scientific research, seeking expert advice, and sharing personal anecdotes. By combining these different sources, I aim to provide a well-rounded understanding of the transformative power of manifestation. Additionally, I will reference relevant theoretical frameworks or models to further enhance the credibility of the claims presented.

The Power of Thoughts:

Thoughts have a profound influence on shaping our reality. Negative thoughts can hinder personal growth and transformation, while positive thoughts can propel us towards our desired outcomes. It is crucial to recognize the power our thoughts hold in determining the trajectory of our lives.

For instance, by changing negative thought patterns and replacing them with positive ones, we can witness positive changes manifesting in various areas of our lives. Our thoughts lay the foundation for our actions and ultimately shape our reality. By consciously cultivating a positive mindset, we can unlock the transformative power of our thoughts.

Manifesting Desires:

The concept of manifesting desires is central to the transformative power discussed in this book. By aligning our thoughts, actions, and intentions with our desired outcomes, we can manifest what we truly desire in life. Techniques such as visualization, affirmation, and gratitude exercises can aid us in this process.

Visualization allows us to create a clear mental image of our desired reality, while affirmation helps to reinforce positive beliefs and intentions. Practicing gratitude cultivates a sense of abundance and attracts more of what we are grateful for into our lives. These techniques serve as powerful tools to align our thoughts and actions with our desired outcomes, enabling us to manifest our deepest desires.

Setting Goals and Taking Action:

Setting goals and taking consistent action towards them is a pivotal aspect of personal transformation. Without clear goals and actionable steps, our desires remain mere aspirations. Effective goal-setting strategies, such as setting SMART goals and creating action plans, provide us with a roadmap towards our desired outcomes.

By consistently taking action towards our goals, we create momentum and set ourselves up for transformative experiences. Each step taken brings us closer to our aspirations, instilling a sense of achievement and fulfillment along the way.

Overcoming Challenges and Obstacles:

On our transformational journey, we may encounter various challenges and obstacles that test our resolve. It is important to acknowledge and prepare for these hurdles. Strategies such as cultivating resilience, seeking support, and reframing setbacks as opportunities for growth can help us overcome these challenges.

By embracing resilience, we can bounce back stronger from setbacks. Seeking support from mentors, friends, or communities can provide guidance and encouragement when facing difficulties. Reframing setbacks as opportunities for growth allows us to view challenges through a positive lens, transforming them into stepping stones towards personal transformation.

Real-Life Success Stories:

Real-life success stories serve as powerful illustrations of the transformative power of the techniques and practices shared in this book. These stories highlight how individuals have manifested their desires and achieved their goals through the power of their thoughts and actions. By witnessing these stories, readers can gain inspiration and belief in their own ability to create transformative experiences.

Conclusion and Next Steps:

In conclusion, this subchapter has provided an introduction to the transformative power of manifestation. We have discussed the significance of terms such as transformative power, techniques, practices, harnessing thoughts, and manifesting desires. By exploring the power of thoughts, the concept of manifesting desires, setting goals and taking action, overcoming challenges and obstacles, and real-life success stories, we have laid the groundwork for personal transformation.

I encourage readers to continue reading and applying the principles shared in this book. The upcoming chapters will delve deeper into specific techniques and practices, providing further guidance and insights for personal transformation. By embracing the transformative power of manifestation, we can embark on a journey of profound growth and create the reality we truly desire.

Chapter 2: The Fundamentals of Manifestation

What Is Manifestation?

Manifestation is a concept that has gained significant attention in recent years, and for good reason. It holds the key to unlocking our desires and goals, allowing us to create the life we truly want. But what exactly is manifestation, and why is it important to explore?

Manifestation can be defined as the process of bringing our desires into physical reality through the power of our thoughts and beliefs. It is the ability to create our own reality by harnessing the power of our mind. This concept may seem abstract or even mystical to some, but it is rooted in the understanding that our thoughts and beliefs shape our experiences.

Our thoughts are incredibly powerful. They are the foundation upon which our reality is built. Every thought we have carries a certain energy and vibration, and these vibrations attract similar energies into our lives. In other words, our thoughts create our reality.

But it's not just our thoughts that play a role in manifestation; our beliefs are equally important. Our beliefs act as filters through which we perceive and interpret the world. They determine what we believe is possible or impossible, and they influence our ability to manifest our desires.

The relationship between our thoughts, beliefs, and manifestation is a powerful one. Our thoughts give rise to our beliefs, and our beliefs shape our thoughts. They work in harmony to create our reality and determine our ability to manifest. If we want to change our reality and manifest our desires, we need to examine and shift our thoughts and beliefs.

One of the biggest obstacles to manifestation is limiting beliefs. These are beliefs that hold us back and prevent us from realizing our full potential. They can be deeply ingrained and can act as barriers to our success. Overcoming these limiting beliefs is crucial if we want to unlock the full power of manifestation.

To overcome limiting beliefs, we must first identify them. This requires self-reflection and an honest assessment of our beliefs. Once we have identified our limiting beliefs, we can then challenge and transform them. This may involve using techniques such as affirmations, visualization, or seeking support from a coach or therapist.

Cultivating positive thoughts and beliefs is equally important for successful manifestation. When we have a positive mindset, we are more likely to attract positive experiences and opportunities into our lives. This can be achieved through practices such as gratitude, positive affirmations, and surrounding ourselves with positive influences.

Emotions also play a crucial role in manifestation. Our emotions are powerful energy magnets that can either align us with our desires or repel them. By consciously aligning our emotions with our desires, we can accelerate the manifestation process and manifest our goals more quickly.

Two techniques that are often used to enhance manifestation abilities are visualization and affirmations. Visualization involves vividly imagining ourselves already having achieved our desired outcome. Affirmations, on the other hand, are positive statements that we repeat to ourselves to reinforce positive beliefs and attract what we desire.

In summary, manifestation is a powerful tool that allows us to create the life we truly want. By harnessing the power of our thoughts, beliefs, emotions, visualization, and affirmations, we can shape our reality and manifest our desires. It requires self-reflection, overcoming limiting beliefs, cultivating positive thoughts and beliefs, and aligning our emotions with our desires. I encourage you to explore and apply the principles of manifestation in your own life and see the transformation that unfolds.

The Power of Thoughts and Beliefs

When it comes to the art of manifestation, there is one fundamental truth that cannot be overlooked: our thoughts and beliefs hold immense power. They are the driving force behind the entire manifestation process, shaping our reality and determining the experiences and circumstances we attract into our lives.

In this subchapter, we will delve deep into the profound influence that our thoughts and beliefs have on the manifestation process. By understanding this influence, we can harness the true power of our minds and unlock our full potential to manifest our desires.

Understanding the Influence of Thoughts on Reality

It is often said that our thoughts create our reality, and this statement holds a profound truth. Every thought we think, consciously or unconsciously, sends out a vibrational frequency into the universe, attracting similar frequencies back to us. In essence, our thoughts become a magnetic force that shapes the experiences and circumstances that manifest in our lives.

Think about it for a moment. Have you ever noticed that when you think positively, you seem to attract positive outcomes? And conversely, when you dwell on negative thoughts, negative situations tend to manifest? This is not mere coincidence; it is the direct result of the vibrational energy we emit through our thoughts.

Examining Limiting Beliefs

While thoughts have the power to shape our reality, they are often influenced by our deeply ingrained beliefs. These beliefs, known as limiting beliefs, act as barriers that hinder our ability to manifest our desires. They are the whispers in our mind that tell us we are not worthy, capable, or deserving of what we truly want.

Limiting beliefs can take many forms, ranging from beliefs about money and success to beliefs about love and relationships. They are often rooted in past experiences, societal conditioning, or negative self-perception. Regardless of their origin, these beliefs have the potential to sabotage our manifestation efforts and keep us stuck in a cycle of unfulfillment.

Techniques to Cultivate Positive Thoughts

To break free from the grip of limiting beliefs and harness the power of thoughts in the manifestation process, we must actively cultivate positive thoughts. By consciously choosing our thoughts and focusing on empowering beliefs, we can shift our vibrational frequency and align ourselves with the desired outcomes we wish to manifest.

One effective technique to cultivate positive thoughts is through the use of affirmations. Affirmations are powerful statements that reinforce positive beliefs and reprogram the subconscious mind. By repeating affirmations regularly, we can override negative thought patterns and replace them with empowering thoughts that support our manifestation journey.

Visualization as a Manifestation Technique

In addition to affirmations, visualization is another potent technique that can help align our thoughts and beliefs with our desired outcomes. Visualization involves vividly imagining ourselves already living and experiencing our desires, as if they have already manifested. This practice not only activates the law of attraction but also enhances our belief in the possibility of our desires coming to fruition.

Challenging Negative Thoughts and Beliefs

To truly harness the power of our thoughts and beliefs, it is crucial to challenge and reframe negative thoughts and beliefs that hold us back. This process involves becoming aware of our negative thought patterns, questioning their validity, and consciously choosing more empowering thoughts.

By challenging our negative thoughts and beliefs, we begin to dismantle the barriers that prevent us from manifesting our desires. We can replace self-doubt with self-confidence, scarcity mindset with abundance mindset, and fear with courage. This transformation allows us to shift towards more empowering thoughts that align with our true potential.

The Role of Self-Talk in Manifestation

One often overlooked aspect of thoughts and beliefs in the manifestation process is our self-talk. Our self-talk refers to the internal dialogue we have with ourselves, the thoughts we think about ourselves, and the beliefs we hold about our abilities and worthiness.

Improving our self-talk is a powerful way to promote positive thinking and reinforce empowering thoughts and beliefs. By consciously choosing words of encouragement, self-compassion, and belief in our abilities, we can cultivate a mindset that supports our manifestation journey.

The Power of Gratitude in Shaping Thoughts and Beliefs

Gratitude is another transformative tool that plays a vital role in shaping our thoughts and beliefs. When we practice gratitude, we shift our focus from lack and scarcity to abundance and appreciation. By acknowledging and appreciating what we already have, we raise our vibrational frequency and attract more positive experiences into our lives.

By regularly expressing gratitude for the present moment and the manifestations that are already unfolding, we cultivate a mindset of positivity and abundance. This mindset, in turn, aligns our thoughts and beliefs with the limitless possibilities of the universe and supports our manifestation efforts.

The Importance of Consistency and Persistence

In the realm of manifestation, consistency and persistence are key. It is not enough to simply have positive thoughts and beliefs sporadically; we must consistently and persistently practice cultivating them.

Consistency and persistence help solidify our new thought patterns and beliefs, making them more ingrained in our subconscious mind. By committing to daily practices such as affirmations, visualization, and gratitude, we reinforce positive thoughts and beliefs, and eventually, they become our default way of thinking.

In conclusion, the power of thoughts and beliefs cannot be underestimated in the manifestation process. They are the driving force behind the reality we create and the experiences we attract into our lives. By understanding and harnessing this power, we can unlock our full potential and manifest our deepest desires. So let us embark on this journey together, exploring the limitless possibilities that lie within the power of our thoughts and beliefs.

The Role of Intention in Manifestation

As I sit down to write about the role of intention in manifestation, I am filled with a sense of excitement and anticipation. This subchapter delves into the profound significance of setting clear intentions for manifestation and explores the concept of aligning intentions with desires. By understanding the power of intention and learning to harness it effectively, we can unlock the ultimate power of manifestation.

Intentions act as a roadmap for manifestation, guiding us towards our desired outcomes. When we set clear and specific intentions, we are able to focus our energy and attention in a directed and purposeful way. This focused intention amplifies the manifestation process, allowing our desires to manifest more quickly and effortlessly.

But it's not just about setting intentions; it's about aligning them with our beliefs and emotions. Our intentions must be in harmony with our deepest beliefs and emotions in order to manifest effectively. If there is a misalignment between our intentions and our beliefs, it can create resistance and hinder the manifestation process.

Clarity and specificity are key when it comes to setting intentions for manifestation. The clearer and more specific we are about what we want to manifest, the easier it becomes for the universe to bring it into our reality. Vague intentions lead to vague manifestations, while specific intentions yield specific and tangible results.

However, there is an unexpected twist to consider - the influence of unconscious intentions on manifestation. Often, our unconscious intentions may conflict with our conscious desires. These hidden intentions can arise from past experiences, limiting beliefs, or fears that we may not even be aware of. They can sabotage our efforts to manifest our desires, acting as an invisible barrier between us and what we truly want.

Uncovering and aligning these unconscious intentions with our conscious desires is essential for successful manifestation. By bringing these hidden intentions to the surface and addressing them, we can clear the path for our conscious intentions to manifest effortlessly. This process requires self-awareness and a willingness to delve into our deepest fears and beliefs, but the rewards are immeasurable.

Understanding and working with unconscious intentions can bring about profound personal growth and transformation. It allows us to release any limiting beliefs or fears that may be holding us back and empowers us to create the life we truly desire. Through self-reflection and introspection, we can align our intentions and desires, paving the way for successful manifestation.

In conclusion, the role of intention in manifestation cannot be overstated. By setting clear and specific intentions, aligning them with our beliefs and emotions, and addressing any unconscious intentions that may be present, we unlock the ultimate power of manifestation. It is through this alignment that we can manifest our desires with ease and create a life of abundance and fulfillment. So, let us embrace the power of intention and watch as our dreams become our reality.

The Connection Between Manifestation and Energy

I believe that the connection between manifestation and energy is one of the most fascinating aspects of the manifestation process. Energy and vibrations play a crucial role in shaping our reality and attracting the manifestations we desire. In this subchapter, I have explored the importance of energy and vibrations in manifestation and how understanding and harnessing these forces can lead to incredible results. To illustrate the relationship between energy and manifestation, let me present a specific case study. Meet Sarah, a young woman who had been struggling with finding a fulfilling career. Despite her best efforts, she couldn't seem to land a job that truly aligned with her passions and skills. Sarah's energy was low, and she constantly felt stuck and frustrated in her current situation. The background of Sarah's case study is crucial in understanding the power of energy in manifestation. She grew up in a household where her parents constantly doubted her abilities and dreams. Their negative energy had a profound impact on her self-confidence and belief in her own potential. As a result, Sarah's energy frequency was consistently low, which attracted similar negative situations into her life. However, everything changed when Sarah started to consciously work on raising her energetic frequency. She began to understand the concept of energy frequency and how it directly related to her manifestations. Sarah realized that by shifting her energy from negative to positive, she could attract the opportunities and experiences she desired. Positive energy, she discovered, had the power to transform her life. When Sarah shifted her focus towards gratitude and self-care, her energy levels began to rise. She started practicing positive affirmations and visualization, which helped her align with her desires and raise her energetic frequency even further. As a result, Sarah started attracting job opportunities that were in alignment with her passions and skills. Sarah's case study exemplifies the significance of vibrational alignment in the manifestation process. When we are in vibrational alignment with our desires, the universe responds by bringing those desires into our reality. Raising our energetic frequency is the key to achieving this alignment. It requires conscious effort and a commitment to self-improvement. There are various techniques that can help individuals raise their energetic frequency. Positive affirmations and visualization are powerful tools in this process. By repeating positive statements and visualizing our desired outcomes, we can reprogram our subconscious mind and align our energy with our manifestations. Practicing gratitude and self-care is another effective technique for increasing energetic frequency. When we express gratitude for the things we already have and take care of ourselves physically, mentally, and emotionally, we create a positive energetic state that attracts more of what we desire. The law of attraction and energetic resonance are intimately connected. Our energetic frequency acts as a magnet, attracting similar frequencies and manifestations into our lives. When we align our energy with our desires, we create a resonance that brings those desires closer to us. It is essential to understand this connection and consciously work on aligning our energy with what we want to manifest. Energetic blocks can hinder our manifestation process. These blocks are the result of past traumas, limiting beliefs, or negative experiences that have left an energetic imprint on us. It is crucial to identify and clear these blocks to allow the free flow of energy and manifestation. Techniques such as energy healing, meditation, and journaling can be helpful in releasing these blocks and creating space for new manifestations. Intuition also plays a vital role in the manifestation process. Our intuition is a powerful guiding force that can lead us towards aligned manifestations. By tapping into and trusting our intuition, we can make decisions that are in alignment with our highest good and attract the experiences we desire. Maintaining a consistently high vibrational energy is essential for manifestation. Strategies such as self-awareness and mindfulness help us manage our energy effectively. By being aware of our thoughts, emotions, and actions, we can make conscious choices that support our energetic frequency. It is also important to protect and preserve our energetic frequency by setting healthy boundaries and surrounding ourselves with positive influences. In conclusion, the connection between manifestation and energy is undeniable. By understanding and harnessing the power of energy and vibrations, we can enhance our manifestation abilities and attract the experiences we desire. I encourage you, the reader, to implement the techniques and concepts discussed in this subchapter to unlock your ultimate power of manifestation.

Chapter 3: Manifestation in Different Areas of Life

Manifesting Abundance and Financial Prosperity

Manifesting abundance and financial prosperity are a concept that has gained significant popularity in recent years. People are increasingly realizing the power of their thoughts and beliefs in attracting wealth and creating a prosperous financial reality. In this book, I aim to guide you through the process of harnessing the ultimate power of manifestation and unlocking your true potential for financial success.

One of the fundamental principles of manifesting abundance is the importance of having a positive mindset and a strong belief in your ability to attract wealth. Your thoughts and beliefs act as a magnet, drawing towards you the financial opportunities and abundance that align with your mindset. By cultivating a positive outlook and developing unwavering belief in your ability to achieve financial success, you can create a powerful foundation for manifesting abundance.

To truly understand the power of manifesting abundance, it is essential to explore the concept of the scarcity mindset. The scarcity mindset is a belief system rooted in the idea that there is a limited number of resources and opportunities available. This mindset can be detrimental to your financial growth, as it limits your ability to recognize and seize opportunities for wealth creation. By identifying and shifting the scarcity mindset, you can open yourself up to a world of financial abundance and unlimited possibilities.

In order to shift the scarcity mindset, there are various techniques that can be employed. Positive affirmations and visualization are powerful tools for changing your beliefs and rewiring your mindset. By consistently affirming positive statements and vividly visualizing your desired financial reality, you can begin to replace limiting beliefs with empowering ones. Additionally, cultivating an attitude of gratitude and embracing an abundance mindset are key to attracting financial prosperity. By focusing on the abundance that already exists in your life and adopting a mindset of abundance, you invite more wealth and opportunities into your life.

Practical steps are also crucial in the manifestation process. Setting clear financial goals and intentions provides a roadmap for achieving financial success. By defining what you want to manifest and taking consistent action towards your goals, you align yourself with the energy of wealth and abundance. It is important to cultivate a positive money mindset and take actions that are in alignment with your financial goals. By staying focused and committed, you can create a prosperous financial reality.

However, it is essential to acknowledge that challenges and obstacles may arise along the journey towards financial prosperity. Self-doubt, fear, and setbacks are common hurdles that can derail your progress. It is important to cultivate perseverance, resilience, and self-belief in order to overcome these challenges. By developing a strong mindset and maintaining unwavering faith in your ability to manifest abundance, you can navigate through any obstacles that come your way.

In conclusion, manifesting abundance and financial prosperity is within your reach. By harnessing the power of your thoughts, beliefs, and actions, you can create a life of financial success and abundance.

Throughout this book, I will provide you with the tools, techniques, and guidance necessary to unlock your ultimate power of manifestation and create the financial reality you desire. Get ready to embark on a transformative journey towards unlimited wealth and abundance.

Manifesting Love and Relationships

When it comes to manifesting love and relationships, the power of manifestation is an incredible tool. Manifestation allows us to attract and cultivate loving and fulfilling relationships in our lives. By understanding and harnessing the power of manifestation, we can create the relationships we desire and deserve.

The Power of Intention:

Setting clear intentions is essential when manifesting love and relationships. Intention acts as the guiding force that shapes the manifestation process and influences the outcomes we experience. By being intentional in our thoughts, actions, and desires, we can align ourselves with the love and relationships we truly want.

Self-Love and Self-Worth:

Self-love and self-worth play a crucial role in manifesting healthy and fulfilling relationships. When we love and value ourselves, we attract partners who also recognize our worth. Cultivating self-love and self-worth involves practices such as self-care, self-reflection, and setting healthy boundaries. By prioritizing our own well-being, we create the foundation for meaningful and lasting connections.

Attracting Love Through Energy and Vibration:

Energy and vibration are fundamental in attracting love and relationships into our lives. By raising our energy and vibration, we become magnetic to the experiences we desire. Practices like visualization and affirmations can help shift our energy and align us with the love we seek. When we radiate positive energy, we naturally draw in loving and compatible partners.

Practicing Gratitude and Appreciation:

Gratitude and appreciation are powerful tools for manifesting love and relationships. By cultivating a mindset of gratitude, we shift our focus towards the abundance of love that surrounds us. Gratitude practices, such as keeping a gratitude journal or expressing appreciation for our partners, help us attract more love and deepen our connections.

Letting Go of Limiting Beliefs and Resistance:

Limiting beliefs and resistance can hinder the manifestation of love and relationships. These negative thought patterns and emotional barriers create blocks in our energetic field, preventing us from attracting what we truly desire. Identifying and releasing limiting beliefs and resistance is a crucial step towards opening ourselves up to love and creating the relationships we deserve.

The Law of Attraction and Alignment:

The law of attraction plays a vital role in manifesting love and relationships. By aligning our thoughts, emotions, and actions with our desires, we become a vibrational match for the love we seek. By focusing on positive thoughts, cultivating loving emotions, and taking inspired action, we align ourselves with the love and relationships that are meant for us.

Building a Supportive and Loving Environment:

Creating a supportive and loving environment is essential for manifesting love and relationships. Surrounding ourselves with positive influences and nurturing relationships sets the stage for healthy connections. By fostering a space of love and support, we attract partners who are aligned with our values and goals.

Practices for Cultivating Healthy Relationships:

Cultivating healthy and fulfilling relationships requires conscious effort and dedication. Effective communication, setting boundaries, and prioritizing self-care are key practices for nurturing healthy connections. Maintaining individuality within relationships and honoring our own needs allows us to grow alongside our partners, creating a strong foundation for love to flourish.

Expanding Love Beyond Romantic Relationships:

Love and fulfilling relationships are not limited to romantic partnerships. They extend to all areas of our lives, including friendships and family relationships. By manifesting love and connection in various relationships, we enrich our lives and create a network of support and love. Practices such as expressing gratitude, active listening, and acts of kindness can deepen our connections beyond romantic love.

In conclusion, the power of manifestation offers us the ability to attract and cultivate loving and fulfilling relationships. By understanding the importance of intention, self-love, energy, gratitude, releasing limiting beliefs, alignment, creating a supportive environment, and practicing healthy relationship habits, we can manifest the love and relationships we desire in all areas of our lives.

Manifesting Health and Well-being

When it comes to manifesting optimal health and well-being, the power lies within our own hands. In this chapter, we will explore the concept of manifesting vibrant health and delve into the mind-body connection, understanding how our thoughts and beliefs can impact our physical well-being. By adopting various techniques and practices, setting clear intentions, embracing a positive mindset, and nurturing supportive relationships, we can embark on a lifelong journey towards vibrant health.

Understanding the Mind-Body Connection:

The relationship between the mind and body is undeniable. Our thoughts, emotions, and beliefs have a profound impact on our physical health. Science has shown that stress, negative thinking, and unresolved emotions can manifest as physical ailments. By understanding this connection, we can harness the power of our minds to support our overall well-being. Through self-reflection and awareness, we can identify the thoughts and beliefs that may be hindering our health and replace them with positive affirmations and empowering beliefs.

Techniques for Boosting Vitality:

Boosting vitality and overall well-being requires a holistic approach. This involves incorporating various practices into our daily lives. Meditation, for example, can calm the mind, reduce stress, and promote relaxation. Exercise is not only beneficial for our physical health but also releases endorphins, enhancing our mood and overall well-being. Nourishing our bodies with nutritious food provides the necessary fuel for optimal functioning. Additionally, self-care and stress management practices, such as deep breathing exercises and engaging in hobbies, play a crucial role in promoting our well-being.

Setting Intentions for Vibrant Health:

The power of intention is a force that can shape our reality. By setting clear and focused intentions for optimal well-being, we can manifest vibrant health. It starts with identifying the areas of our health that require improvement and envisioning our desired state of well-being.

Daily affirmations and visualization techniques can be incorporated into our routine to reinforce these intentions and support the manifestation of vibrant health. By consistently aligning our thoughts, emotions, and actions with our intentions, we can create a powerful momentum towards our desired state of well-being.

The Role of Positive Thinking:

Positive thinking has a profound impact on our health and well-being. Cultivating a positive mindset can promote healing and resilience, enabling us to overcome challenges with grace. By reframing negative thoughts and focusing on gratitude and positivity, we can shift our energy towards attracting positive experiences and outcomes. It is through the power of our thoughts that we can create a foundation of well-being and open ourselves up to limitless possibilities.

Embracing a Holistic Approach:

To truly manifest vibrant health, we must embrace a holistic approach. This means addressing not only the physical aspects of our health but also the emotional and spiritual dimensions. By nurturing all aspects of our being, we create a harmonious balance that supports our overall well-being. Integrating alternative therapies and practices, such as acupuncture, energy healing, and mindfulness, can further enhance our wellness routine and provide additional tools for self-care and self-improvement.

The Power of Self-Reflection:

Self-reflection is a powerful tool for maintaining optimal health. By taking the time to journal and assess ourselves, we can identify areas for growth and improvement. This process allows us to gain a deeper understanding of our needs, desires, and aspirations, ultimately leading to greater self-compassion and forgiveness. By embracing self-reflection as a regular practice, we can navigate our journey towards vibrant health with self-awareness and intention.

Nurturing Supportive Relationships:

The impact of relationships on our health and well-being cannot be overstated. Cultivating supportive and nurturing relationships provides a sense of connection, love, and support that is essential for our overall well-being. Setting boundaries, expressing our needs, and seeking social connection can enhance our mental and emotional health. By surrounding ourselves with individuals who uplift and inspire us, we create a positive environment that fosters our growth and well-being.

Creating a Healthy Environment:

Our physical environment plays a significant role in our health and well-being. By decluttering, organizing, and creating a space that supports our well-being, we can enhance our overall vitality. Incorporating elements of nature, such as plants and natural light, can improve our mood and increase our sense of well-being. Creating a healthy environment extends beyond our physical space to include the people, activities, and experiences we surround ourselves with. By consciously curating a supportive environment, we can further manifest vibrant health.

Maintaining Consistency and Persistence:

Consistency and persistence are key to manifesting health and well-being. Establishing healthy habits and routines requires commitment and dedication. By consistently engaging in practices that support our well-being, we create a foundation for long-lasting vitality. It is important to overcome obstacles and stay motivated on this journey. By cultivating resilience and tapping into our inner strength, we can navigate challenges and setbacks with unwavering determination.

Embracing a Lifelong Journey:

Manifesting health and well-being are not a destination; it is a lifelong journey. It requires continuous learning, growth, and adaptation. Embracing self-care and self-improvement as ongoing practices allows us to evolve and expand our understanding of what it means to be truly healthy. As we navigate through life's ups and downs, we can embrace the challenges as opportunities for growth and transformation. By committing to our well-being, we embark on a lifelong journey towards vibrant health, knowing that we have the power to manifest our own destiny.

Manifesting Success and Career Growth

In this subchapter, we will explore the powerful concept of manifestation in the context of success and career growth. Understanding how manifestation can influence our professional lives is crucial for achieving our goals and finding fulfillment in our careers. By harnessing the power of manifestation, we can attract opportunities, overcome obstacles, and ultimately achieve the level of success we desire.

Defining Terms:

Manifestation is the process of bringing our desires and goals into reality through focused intention and belief. When applied to success and career growth, manifestation involves using our thoughts, emotions, and actions to attract the opportunities and outcomes that align with our professional aspirations. By adopting a mindset of abundance and actively visualizing our desired outcomes, we can consciously manifest success in our careers.

Objectives and Scope:

The main goals of this subchapter are to help readers clarify their career goals, attract opportunities, and achieve professional success. We will delve into various topics that are essential for this journey, including goal setting, visualization techniques, and cultivating a positive mindset. By covering a range of subjects, we aim to provide a comprehensive guide that empowers individuals to manifest their career aspirations.

Methodology and Approach:

In this subchapter, we will employ research-based strategies and draw from expert advice to present effective methods for manifesting success and career growth. By incorporating both practical techniques and theoretical frameworks, we aim to provide readers with a well-rounded approach to manifestation. This multifaceted approach will enable individuals to leverage the power of manifestation in their professional lives.

Clarifying Career Goals:

To manifest success in our careers, it is crucial to have clear and specific goals. We will explore strategies for clarifying career goals, including self-reflection exercises and goal-setting techniques. By gaining a deeper understanding of our passions, values, and long-term aspirations, we can align our actions with our desired outcomes and increase the likelihood of achieving professional success.

Attracting Opportunities:

Manifestation can be a powerful tool for attracting opportunities that align with our career goals. In this section, we will discuss techniques such as networking, building relationships, and creating a personal brand. By consciously manifesting our desired opportunities, we can position ourselves to attract the right connections, projects, and collaborations that will propel us towards success.

Achieving Professional Success:

Manifestation can also help us overcome obstacles and achieve career milestones. We will explore strategies for achieving professional success, including developing skills and knowledge, seeking mentorship, and taking calculated risks. By harnessing the power of manifestation, we can cultivate the resilience, determination, and resourcefulness necessary for overcoming challenges and reaching our full potential.

Visualization Techniques:

Visualization is a powerful manifestation technique that involves creating vivid mental images of our desired outcomes. In this section, we will explain the role of visualization in manifesting success and career growth. Additionally, we will provide instruction on how to effectively visualize our career goals and desired outcomes. By consistently visualizing our success, we can strengthen our belief in achieving our goals and attract the necessary resources and opportunities to make them a reality.

Positive Mindset:

Maintaining a positive mindset is crucial for manifesting success and career growth. In this section, we will discuss the importance of cultivating a positive mindset and provide techniques for doing so. These techniques may include affirmations, gratitude practices, and self-care strategies. By consciously cultivating positivity, we can shift our thoughts and emotions towards success and create a fertile ground for manifestation.

Overcoming Limiting Beliefs:

Limiting beliefs can hinder our progress and limit our potential for success. In this section, we will explore common limiting beliefs that may arise in the pursuit of career growth. Additionally, we will provide strategies for identifying and overcoming these beliefs through manifestation. By challenging and transforming our limiting beliefs, we can pave the way for unlimited growth and achieve the professional success we desire.

Case Studies and Examples:

To illustrate the concepts and strategies discussed in this subchapter, we will include case studies and real-life examples of individuals who have successfully used manifestation techniques to achieve career growth. These stories will serve as inspiration and provide practical insights into how manifestation can be applied in different professional contexts. By learning from the experiences of others, readers can gain valuable perspectives and apply these strategies to their own careers.

Incorporating Action Steps:

Finally, we will provide guidance on how to incorporate the strategies and techniques discussed into daily practice. By creating an action plan for manifesting success and career growth, readers can take practical steps towards their desired outcomes. We will offer instruction on setting goals, developing a routine, and maintaining accountability. By implementing these action steps consistently, individuals can actively manifest their professional aspirations and create the career they truly desire.

Chapter 4: Preparing Yourself for Manifestation

Cultivating a Positive Mindset

Positive thinking is a concept that has been widely discussed and celebrated in the realm of self-help and personal development. It is the idea that our thoughts and beliefs have a profound impact on our mindset, which in turn shapes our reality. When we adopt a positive mindset, we are able to approach challenges and setbacks with resilience and optimism.

The benefits of cultivating a positive mindset are far-reaching. Not only does it improve our mental and emotional well-being, but it also enhances our overall quality of life. Research has shown that individuals with a positive mindset experience reduced stress levels, improved relationships, and increased productivity. By choosing to focus on the positive aspects of life, we are able to create a virtuous cycle of positivity and abundance.

Recognizing Negative Thought Patterns

However, before we can fully embrace the power of positive thinking, it is essential to recognize and address the negative thought patterns that often hold us back. These negative thought patterns can take many forms, such as self-doubt, negative self-talk, and limiting beliefs. They have a detrimental effect on our mindset and overall well-being, often leading to feelings of anxiety, self-sabotage, and a sense of powerlessness.

Shifting Negative Thought Patterns

Fortunately, there are techniques and strategies that can help us shift these negative thought patterns and cultivate a more positive mindset. The first step is to develop awareness and mindfulness around our thoughts. By paying attention to our internal dialogue, we can begin to challenge and reframe negative beliefs. This process requires practice and patience, but it is essential in creating lasting change.

Positive affirmations and visualization techniques are also effective tools in shifting negative thought patterns. By consciously choosing to focus on positive statements and imagery, we can rewire our brains to see opportunities instead of obstacles. It is important to remember that this is an ongoing practice, and it may take time to fully reprogram our thought patterns.

Creating a Positive Environment

In addition to addressing our internal thought patterns, it is equally important to consider the influence of our external environment. Our surroundings play a significant role in shaping our mindset and can either support or hinder our efforts to cultivate positivity. To create a positive environment, we can surround ourselves with like-minded individuals who uplift and inspire us. Engaging in activities that bring us joy and practicing gratitude on a daily basis can also contribute to a positive mindset.

Building Self-Confidence

Self-confidence is a key component of a positive mindset. When we believe in ourselves and our abilities, we are more likely to take risks and overcome challenges. To build self-confidence, it is important to set achievable goals and celebrate small victories along the way. Taking care of ourselves through self-care practices, such as exercise, mindfulness, and nourishing our bodies, also helps to boost self-confidence.

Practicing Positive Self-Talk

Our internal dialogue, or self-talk, has a significant impact on our mindset. By practicing positive self-talk, we can reframe negative beliefs and cultivate a more empowering mindset. This can be achieved by challenging negative thoughts and replacing them with positive, empowering beliefs. Focusing on our strengths and past achievements can also help to reinforce a positive self-image.

Developing Resilience

Resilience is another important aspect of maintaining a positive mindset. Life is filled with challenges and setbacks, but it is our ability to bounce back and learn from these experiences that ultimately determines our mindset. Embracing challenges as opportunities for growth, learning from failures, and seeking support when needed are all strategies that can help us develop resilience.

Cultivating a Growth Mindset

A growth mindset is closely connected to a positive mindset. It is the belief that our abilities and intelligence can be developed through effort and practice. By embracing learning opportunities, seeking feedback, and reframing failures as opportunities for growth, we can cultivate a growth mindset. This mindset allows us to approach life with curiosity and optimism, knowing that we have the power to learn and improve.

Finding Purpose and Meaning

Lastly, finding purpose and meaning in life is crucial for maintaining a positive mindset. When we have a clear sense of our passions and values, we are more likely to approach life with a sense of purpose and fulfillment. Strategies such as exploring new interests, setting meaningful goals, and aligning our actions with our values can help us discover and pursue our purpose.

Maintaining a Positive Mindset

In conclusion, cultivating a positive mindset is an ongoing practice that requires commitment and effort. By recognizing and challenging negative thought patterns, creating a positive environment, building self-confidence, practicing positive self-talk, developing resilience, cultivating a growth mindset, and finding purpose and meaning, we can maintain a positive mindset in our daily lives. It is through this commitment to positivity that we can unlock the ultimate power of manifestation and create a life filled with joy, abundance, and success.

Clearing Limiting Beliefs

As I delve into the fascinating world of manifestation, I can't help but be drawn to the concept of limiting beliefs and their impact on our ability to manifest our desires. Our beliefs have the power to shape our reality, either supporting or hindering the manifestation process. Let me paint a hypothetical scenario for you to better understand how these beliefs can influence our lives.

Imagine a woman named Sarah. Like many of us, Sarah has a burning desire to manifest financial abundance. She dreams of a life filled with financial freedom, where she can pursue her passions and live a life of purpose. However, despite her best efforts, Sarah consistently faces obstacles and setbacks on her path to abundance.

Upon closer examination, it becomes clear that Sarah's self-limiting beliefs about money and abundance are holding her back. Deep-rooted beliefs of scarcity and lack have taken hold of her subconscious mind, creating a mindset that attracts more of the same into her life. This scenario is not uncommon, as many of us unknowingly harbor these self-limiting beliefs that act as barriers to our manifestation journey.

But why do we hold onto these beliefs that limit our potential? The assumptions, conditions, and relevance of this scenario lie in the fact that these beliefs often stem from childhood experiences, societal conditioning, and negative past experiences. Sarah may have grown up in a household where money was seen as scarce, or she may have faced financial struggles in her past. These experiences have shaped her beliefs about money and abundance, causing her to operate from a place of lack rather than abundance.

Identifying and Understanding Limiting Beliefs:

To truly harness the power of manifestation, it is crucial to identify and understand our limiting beliefs. These beliefs often operate on a subconscious level, making them difficult to recognize and overcome. However, with the right tools and practices, we can bring these beliefs to the surface and transform them.

One effective tool for uncovering limiting beliefs is journaling. By writing down our thoughts, fears, and doubts, we can gain insight into the beliefs that may be holding us back. Self-reflection is another powerful practice that allows us to explore our inner world and uncover hidden beliefs that may be influencing our reality.

In addition to these practices, working with a coach or therapist can provide valuable guidance and support on our journey of self-discovery. They can help us navigate through the layers of our beliefs, challenging us to question their validity and empowering us to let go of what no longer serves us.

As we embark on this journey of uncovering limiting beliefs, it's important to recognize common themes and patterns. Beliefs related to worthiness, deservingness, and scarcity mindset are often recurring themes that hinder our manifestation efforts. For example, Sarah may hold a belief that she is not worthy of financial abundance, or that there is never enough to go around. These beliefs create a barrier between her and her desired manifestations, perpetuating a cycle of lack.

Challenging and Overcoming Limiting Beliefs:

Now that we have identified our limiting beliefs, it is time to challenge and overcome them. Shifting our beliefs is the key to opening up new possibilities and aligning ourselves with our desired manifestations.

Affirmations are a powerful tool for challenging and transforming limiting beliefs. By repeating positive statements that counteract our negative beliefs, we can reprogram our subconscious mind and create new neural pathways. Visualization is another technique that allows us to vividly imagine ourselves living our desired reality, effectively rewiring our brains to support our manifestations.

To overcome limiting beliefs, we must also cultivate self-compassion and self-acceptance. It is essential to recognize that we are not defined by our past beliefs or experiences. By embracing a loving mindset towards ourselves, we can release the grip of self-judgment and move towards a place of growth and expansion.

However, it's important to acknowledge that resistance and fear may arise when challenging and letting go of limiting beliefs. Our subconscious mind is wired to resist change, even if it is for our own good. To navigate through this resistance, we can employ strategies such as mindfulness, meditation, and emotional release techniques. By staying present and acknowledging our fears, we can move past them and cultivate a mindset of abundance and possibility.

Integration and Continued Practice:

Clearing limiting beliefs is not a one-time event, but rather a lifelong practice. It requires consistent self-reflection, awareness, and commitment to maintaining empowering beliefs. As we continue on this journey, we must make it a priority to nurture and cultivate our mindset, just as we would tend to a garden.

The integration of empowering beliefs into our lives has a ripple effect, extending beyond the realm of manifestation. By releasing these limiting beliefs, we open ourselves up to personal growth, improved relationships, and overall well-being. Our newfound mindset of abundance and possibility permeates every aspect of our lives, creating a profound shift in our reality.

Practical Examples and Success Stories:

To further illustrate the transformative power of clearing limiting beliefs, let's explore some practical examples and success stories. These individuals have successfully shifted their beliefs and manifested their desires, proving that anyone can do the same with the right mindset and actions.

One inspiring story is that of John, who struggled with a belief that he was not deserving of success. Through deep self-reflection and working with a coach, he was able to identify this limiting belief and challenge its validity. With affirmations, visualization, and consistent action, John was able to manifest his dream job and create a life of abundance and fulfillment.

Another example is the case of Sarah, our hypothetical scenario. Through the process of uncovering and challenging her self-limiting beliefs, she was able to release her fear of scarcity and embrace a mindset of abundance. As a result, Sarah attracted new opportunities, financial abundance, and a sense of purpose in her life.

In conclusion, the power of clearing limiting beliefs and aligning with our true potential is truly transformative. By recognizing and challenging these beliefs, we can manifest our desires and create a life of abundance and fulfillment. It is within each of us to harness the ultimate power of manifestation, and it all begins with our beliefs. So, I invite you to embark on this journey with me and discover the extraordinary possibilities that await.

Creating a Vision for Your Life

Creating a vision for one's life is a vital component of personal growth and fulfillment. It serves as a roadmap, providing clarity and direction for our actions and decisions. As I delved into the existing literature on visualization techniques and their impact on achieving goals, I was amazed by the profound effects that visualization can have on manifesting our desired outcomes. This subchapter aims to guide readers in the process of creating a compelling vision for their lives.

The Power of Visualization:

Visualization, simply put, is the process of mentally creating a clear and detailed image of our desired outcome. It has been proven time and again to be a powerful tool in manifesting our goals. Numerous scientific studies have substantiated the effectiveness of visualization, showing that it activates the same neural pathways as actual experiences. By vividly visualizing our goals, we activate our subconscious mind and harness the power of our thoughts and emotions to align our actions with our desired outcomes.

Various visualization techniques exist, each with its own unique approach. Guided imagery, for instance, involves using our imagination to create a sensory-rich mental landscape that vividly depicts our desired reality. Vision boards, on the other hand, employ visual representations of our goals, serving as constant reminders of what we aspire to achieve. By incorporating these techniques into our daily lives, we can enhance our ability to manifest our desires.

Setting Clear Goals:

In the pursuit of creating a compelling vision for our lives, setting clear goals is of utmost importance. The SMART goal-setting framework provides a structured approach to goal setting that increases our chances of success. Each goal should be specific, measurable, achievable, relevant, and time-bound. By ensuring that our goals are well-defined and aligned with our vision, we establish a clear path towards their achievement.

Identifying Values and Passions:

To truly create a vision that resonates with us on a deep level, it is crucial to identify our personal values and passions. Engaging in self-reflection exercises allows us to uncover our core values and passions, giving us insight into what truly matters to us. When our vision aligns with our values and passions, we experience a greater sense of fulfillment and purpose in our lives.

Creating a Vivid Vision:

Creating a vivid vision requires us to delve into the intricate details of our desired reality. By visualizing and describing each aspect of our vision in vivid detail, we bring it to life in our minds. We consider various aspects such as our relationships, career, and personal growth, painting a picture of what our ideal life looks like. By investing time and energy into creating a vivid vision, we strengthen our connection to it and increase our commitment to its realization.

Visualizing Obstacles and Solutions:

Acknowledging potential obstacles on our journey towards our vision is a crucial step in preparing ourselves for the challenges ahead. By visualizing these obstacles and brainstorming potential solutions, we equip ourselves with the tools necessary to overcome them. This exercise not only helps us develop resilience and resourcefulness, but also enhances our ability to adapt and stay focused on our vision.

Implementing Visualization Techniques:

Incorporating visualization techniques into our daily routines and practices is essential for harnessing the full power of manifestation. There are various visualization techniques and exercises that can be used, such as meditation, journaling, or creating a vision board. By making consistent visualization practice a part of our daily lives, we reinforce our commitment to our vision and enhance our ability to manifest our desired outcomes.

Staying Motivated and Committed:

Maintaining motivation and commitment to our vision is crucial for its realization. Strategies such as affirmations, gratitude, and accountability play a pivotal role in this process. Affirmations help us reprogram our subconscious mind, replacing self-doubt with positive beliefs. Expressing gratitude for the progress made along our journey keeps us focused on the positive aspects of our vision. Lastly, having an accountability system, whether it be a mentor, coach, or support group, helps keep us on track and overcome setbacks.

Refining and Updating the Vision:

Regularly reviewing and refining our vision is essential as our lives evolve and circumstances change. Personal growth and life experiences may require adjustments to our vision. By regularly evaluating the alignment of our vision with our current values and passions, we ensure that it remains relevant and meaningful to us.

Putting the Vision into Action:

Creating a vision is only the first step; taking action towards its realization is where the magic happens. By setting milestones, creating action plans, and tracking our progress, we transform our vision into tangible results. As we implement our vision in our daily lives, we experience a greater sense of purpose and fulfillment, as each action brings us closer to our desired reality.

In conclusion, creating a compelling vision for our lives through visualization techniques is a powerful tool for manifesting our goals. By setting clear goals, identifying our values and passions, and creating a vivid vision, we align our actions with our desired outcomes. Visualizing obstacles and solutions, implementing visualization techniques, and staying motivated and committed are essential steps in the manifestation process. Regularly refining and updating our vision ensures its alignment with our evolving values and passions. Finally, putting our vision into action through strategic planning and consistent effort brings us one step closer to living a purposeful and fulfilling life.

Setting Achievable Goals

Setting achievable goals is a crucial aspect of manifesting our desires. It provides us with a roadmap to follow, helping us stay focused and motivated throughout the manifestation process. By setting clear and attainable goals, we can turn our dreams into reality.

Before we can set goals, it is important to understand and clarify our personal desires. This requires taking the time to reflect on what truly matters to us and identifying our priorities. By gaining a deeper understanding of our desires, we can ensure that our goals align with what we truly want to manifest in our lives.

Once we have a clear understanding of our desires, it is essential to set realistic and specific goals. Setting vague or unrealistic goals can lead to frustration and lack of progress. By defining our goals in a measurable and attainable way, we can set ourselves up for success. For example, instead of setting a goal to "lose weight," we can set a specific goal of losing 10 pounds in three months.

Breaking down our goals into actionable steps is another crucial aspect of goal-setting. This process involves identifying the smaller tasks and milestones that will lead us towards achieving our goals. By setting deadlines for these steps, we can stay on track and monitor our progress along the way. Breaking down our goals into manageable chunks makes them feel more attainable and helps us stay motivated.

Creating a goal-setting action plan is a step-by-step process that helps us stay organized and focused on our goals. It involves outlining our goals, the specific action steps required to achieve them, and setting deadlines for each step. By having a clear plan in place, we can eliminate confusion and ensure that we are taking consistent action towards our desired manifestations.

Visualizing success and manifestations are a powerful tool that can help us stay motivated and focused on our goals. By regularly visualizing ourselves achieving our goals and experiencing the desired outcomes, we create a sense of belief and confidence within ourselves. Visualization allows us to tap into the power of our subconscious mind, reinforcing our commitment to our goals and enhancing our manifestation efforts.

Monitoring our progress and making adjustments along the way is crucial for ensuring that we stay on track towards our goals. Regularly assessing our progress allows us to identify areas for improvement and make necessary adjustments to our action plan. It is important to be flexible and adaptable in our approach, as we may encounter obstacles or unforeseen circumstances along the way.

Staying motivated throughout the goal-setting process can be challenging, but it is essential for success. By finding ways to stay inspired, such as surrounding ourselves with supportive individuals or regularly reminding ourselves of the reasons why we are pursuing our goals, we can maintain a high level of motivation. Additionally, developing strategies for overcoming challenges and staying focused during difficult times is crucial for staying on track towards our desired manifestations.

Celebrating our achievements and acknowledging personal growth is an important part of the goal-setting process. By taking the time to acknowledge and celebrate our progress, we reinforce our belief in our abilities and boost our motivation. Rewarding ourselves for reaching milestones or reflecting on our accomplishments can provide us with the encouragement we need to continue pursuing our goals.

Finally, it is essential to regularly reassess our goals and ensure that they remain aligned with our desired manifestations. As we grow and evolve, our desires may change, and it is important to adjust our goals accordingly. By regularly evaluating our goals and making necessary adjustments, we can ensure that our goals are in alignment with our desired manifestations and continue on the path to success.

Chapter 5: Techniques for Manifestation

Visualization: Creating Your Desired Reality

Visualization is a powerful tool when it comes to manifesting our desired outcomes. It allows us to create detailed mental images of the future we want to bring into reality. By visualizing these desired outcomes with clarity and specificity, we can harness the power of our minds to make them a reality.

In this section, I will introduce you to the concept of visualization and its role in manifestation. I will explain how visualization works and why it is such an effective technique for achieving our goals. By the end of this chapter, you will have a clear understanding of what visualization is and what you can expect to learn from this subchapter.

The Process of Visualization

Now that we understand the power of visualization, let's dive into the process itself. I will guide you step-by-step on how to effectively visualize your desired outcomes. This includes techniques for enhancing your visualizations by incorporating your senses and emotions. We will also discuss the importance of clarity and specificity in your visualizations.

Visualization is not just about imagining your desired outcomes; it is about experiencing them as if they were already real. Through visualization, you can tap into the emotions and sensations that come with achieving your goals. This not only enhances the manifestation process but also helps you align your mindset and belief system with your desired reality.

Manifesting Your Desired Reality

Visualization is not just a theoretical concept; it can lead to tangible results in reality. In this section, I will share examples of success stories from individuals who have used visualization techniques to manifest their desired outcomes. These stories will inspire and motivate you to apply visualization in your own life.

We will also discuss the mindset and belief system needed for effective manifestation. It is essential to believe in the power of visualization and to have faith in the process. By cultivating a positive mindset and adopting empowering beliefs, you can accelerate the manifestation of your desired reality.

Overcoming Challenges and Obstacles

While visualization is a powerful tool, it is not without its challenges. In this section, we will address common obstacles that may arise during the visualization process and strategies for overcoming them. I will provide tips for maintaining focus and belief in the face of setbacks or doubts.

Resistance and blocks can hinder the manifestation process. We will explore techniques for overcoming these obstacles and staying on track with your visualization practice. By developing resilience and a strong belief in your abilities, you can overcome any challenges that come your way.

Amplifying the Power of Visualization

In addition to visualization, there are other techniques that can amplify its power. In this section, we will explore the use of affirmations, vision boards, and guided visualizations. These techniques can further enhance the effectiveness of your visualization practice.

I will provide tips for integrating visualization into your daily routines for maximum impact. By incorporating visualization into your daily life, you can create a habit of aligning your thoughts and actions with your desired outcomes. This will help you stay focused and motivated on your manifestation journey.

Integrating Visualization into Everyday Life

Visualization is not just a practice to be done in isolation; it can be integrated into your everyday life. In this section, I will provide guidance on how to incorporate visualization practices into your daily routines. This includes creating a supportive environment for visualization and establishing rituals and habits that reinforce your visualization techniques.

By making visualization a part of your daily life, you will strengthen your manifestation practice and make it more sustainable. It will become second nature to visualize your desired outcomes, and you will effortlessly align your thoughts and actions with your goals.

Fine-Tuning Your Visualization Practice

As you continue to practice visualization, you can refine and fine-tune your skills. In this section, I will share strategies for improving your visualization techniques. This includes exploring different approaches to visualization, such as guided meditation or scripting.

I will provide tips for adapting visualization techniques to your individual preferences and needs. It is important to find a visualization method that resonates with you and allows you to fully immerse yourself in the experience. By continuously refining your visualization practice, you can enhance its effectiveness and accelerate your manifestation journey.

Measuring and Celebrating Progress

Tracking and measuring your progress in manifestation is crucial for staying motivated and making adjustments as needed. In this section, we will discuss the importance of evaluating and adjusting your visualization techniques. I will provide suggestions for measuring your progress and celebrating your small wins along the way.

By acknowledging and celebrating your achievements, no matter how small, you will create a positive feedback loop that reinforces your manifestation practice. This will keep you motivated and inspired to continue on your journey towards manifesting your desired reality.

Deepening the Connection between Visualization and Reality

To deepen the connection between visualization and reality, it is important to align your thoughts, emotions, and actions with your desired outcomes. In this section, I will explore techniques for cultivating a stronger connection between visualization and reality. This includes the role of gratitude and appreciation in the manifestation process.

By expressing gratitude for what you already have and appreciating the progress you have made, you will attract more of the same into your life. This will create a positive energy that aligns with your desired reality and accelerates the manifestation process.

Sustaining and Evolving Your Visualization Practice

Maintaining a consistent visualization practice over time is key to sustaining your manifestation journey. In this section, I will provide advice on how to stay committed to your visualization practice. I will also suggest ways to evolve and expand your visualization techniques as your goals and desires change.

It is important to adapt your visualization practice to align with your evolving needs and desires. By continually exploring and experimenting with visualization, you can ensure ongoing growth and manifestation in your life.

Conclusion

Visualization is a powerful manifestation technique that can transform your life. By harnessing the power of your mind and creating detailed mental images of your desired outcomes, you can bring them into reality. Through the step-by-step guidance and strategies provided in this book, you will become a master of visualization and unlock the ultimate power of manifestation. Get ready to manifest the life of your dreams.

Affirmations: Harnessing the Power of Positive Statements

Affirmations are a powerful tool that has the ability to transform our thoughts and beliefs. They serve as positive statements that we repeat to ourselves in order to reprogram our subconscious mind. By using affirmations, we can shift our mindset and manifest the life we desire. In this chapter, we will explore the importance of affirmations and how they can help us achieve our goals.

Understanding the Subconscious Mind

To truly understand the power of affirmations, it is crucial to grasp the concept of the subconscious mind. Our subconscious mind plays a significant role in shaping our beliefs and behaviors. Unfortunately, negative programming in the subconscious can hinder our personal growth and manifestation abilities. However, by reprogramming our subconscious through affirmations, we can overcome these limitations and create positive change in our lives.

Creating Effective Affirmations

Creating effective affirmations is an art that requires careful consideration. It is essential to craft statements that resonate with our personal goals and desires. By using present tense, positive language, and emotional resonance, we can enhance the effectiveness of our affirmations. This step-by-step guide will help us create powerful affirmations that align with our aspirations.

The Role of Repetition and Consistency

Repetition and consistency are key elements in affirmations. By consistently repeating our affirmations, we reinforce new beliefs and overwrite old patterns. It is important to incorporate affirmations into our daily routines and practices to ensure consistency. This section will introduce various techniques for integrating affirmations into our lives and maximizing their impact.

Visualization and Affirmations

Visualization is a powerful tool that can enhance the power of affirmations. By combining affirmations with vivid mental imagery, we can strengthen the manifestation process. This section will explore the role of visualization and provide techniques that can be used in conjunction with affirmations. Through visualization, we can create a clear picture of our desired outcomes and increase our chances of manifesting them.

Overcoming Resistance and Self-Doubt

Using affirmations can be challenging at times, especially when faced with resistance and self-doubt. However, there are strategies that can help us overcome these obstacles and build belief in the effectiveness of affirmations. This section will provide tips for addressing negative thoughts and limiting beliefs that may arise during the affirmation process. By addressing these challenges head-on, we can stay on track towards our goals.

Affirmations for Specific Goals and Desires

Affirmations can be tailored to address specific goals, desires, and areas of life. Whether it is health, relationships, career, or abundance, affirmations can be customized to align with our personal aspirations and intentions. This section will provide examples of affirmations for various areas and offer tips for personalizing them to fit our unique needs.

Affirmations and Emotional Healing

In addition to manifesting our desires, affirmations can also be used as a tool for emotional healing and personal growth. They have the power to release negative emotions and cultivate positive feelings. This section will explore how affirmations can aid in emotional healing and inner peace. By incorporating affirmations that target emotional healing, we can accelerate our personal growth journey.

Affirmations and Manifestation

Affirmations play a crucial role in the manifestation process. They help us align our thoughts, beliefs, and actions with our desired outcomes. This section will explain how affirmations work in the process of manifestation and provide examples of affirmations that focus on attracting specific manifestations and experiences. By consistently practicing affirmations, we can manifest our dreams into reality.

Daily Affirmation Practice

Establishing a daily affirmation practice is essential for optimal results. By integrating affirmations into our daily routines, we make them a consistent part of our lives. This section will provide guidance on creating a daily affirmation practice and offer tips for staying committed and persistent. Consistency is key, and by making affirmations a habit, we can experience long-term transformation.

Conclusion

Affirmations are a powerful tool that can transform our lives. By understanding the concept of affirmations and their impact on the subconscious mind, we can create effective statements that align with our goals. Through repetition, consistency, visualization, and addressing resistance, we can overcome obstacles and manifest our desires. With affirmations, we have the ultimate power to shape our reality and create the life we truly desire.

Meditation: Aligning Your Mind and Spirit

Meditation is a transformative practice that has the power to align the mind and spirit, enabling us to manifest our deepest desires. It is a tool that can help us achieve inner balance and clarity, providing the foundation for a life of abundance and fulfillment.

When we engage in meditation, we create a sacred space within ourselves where we can connect with our true essence and tap into the infinite potential of the universe. Through this practice, we learn to quiet the noise of the outside world and cultivate a deep sense of presence and awareness.

Different Meditation Techniques:

There are various meditation techniques that can be used to align the mind and spirit. Mindfulness meditation, for example, is a practice that involves bringing our attention to the present moment without judgment. By cultivating present-moment awareness, we are able to reduce stress and enhance our overall well-being.

Guided visualization, another powerful technique, allows us to vividly imagine and create a mental picture of our desired outcomes. By visualizing our goals and desires with great clarity and intensity, we are able to attract them into our reality. This technique is particularly effective in manifesting specific desires and goals.

Loving-kindness meditation, on the other hand, promotes compassion and positive energy. By directing loving-kindness towards ourselves and others, we cultivate a sense of interconnectedness and unity. This practice not only enhances our own well-being, but also contributes to the well-being of those around us.

The Importance of Mindfulness:

Mindfulness plays a crucial role in the manifestation process. When we are fully present in the moment, we are able to enhance our clarity and focus. We become aware of our thoughts, emotions, and sensations, and gain insight into the patterns and beliefs that may be holding us back.

By practicing mindfulness, we can recognize and release negative thought patterns and replace them with positive and empowering ones. This shift in mindset is essential for aligning the mind and spirit and creating a fertile ground for manifestation.

Connecting Mind and Spirit:

The mind and spirit are deeply interconnected, and aligning them is essential for manifesting our desires. Through meditation, we bridge the gap between the conscious and subconscious mind, allowing us to access our full potential and tap into the wisdom of our inner being.

When the mind and spirit are in harmony, we are able to tap into the universal energy that is constantly conspiring to support us. We become co-creators of our reality, able to manifest our desires with greater ease and grace.

The Power of Visualization:

Visualization is a key aspect of meditation that aids in manifestation. When we vividly imagine our desired outcomes, we activate the creative power of our mind and align ourselves with the frequencies of abundance and success.

It is important to believe in the possibilities portrayed through visualization. By cultivating a deep sense of faith and trust, we open ourselves up to receiving the manifestations we desire. Visualization is a powerful tool that allows us to align our thoughts, emotions, and actions with our desired outcomes, bringing them into fruition.

Cultivating Gratitude:

Gratitude is a powerful force that aligns the mind and spirit for manifestation. By practicing gratitude, we shift our focus from lack to abundance, and from negativity to positivity. We become aware of the blessings and opportunities that surround us, and attract more of them into our lives.

Expressing gratitude enhances the manifestation process by raising our energetic frequency and aligning us with the vibration of what we desire. When we are grateful for what we have, we create a magnetic field that attracts more of the same. Gratitude is a transformative practice that has the power to shift our perception and open us up to infinite possibilities.

Overcoming Resistance and Doubt:

Resistance and doubt are common obstacles that can hinder the manifestation process. Through meditation, we can overcome these challenges by cultivating a deep sense of self-belief and trust in the process.

Regular meditation practice strengthens our belief in the manifestation process. It allows us to connect with our inner wisdom and tap into the infinite power that resides within us. By consistently aligning the mind and spirit, we develop a strong foundation for manifestation and overcome any doubts or resistance that may arise.

Maintaining Consistency:

Consistency is key in aligning the mind and spirit for manifestation. By maintaining a regular meditation practice, we create a strong foundation for our desires to manifest. Just as a daily practice of physical exercise strengthens our muscles, a daily practice of meditation strengthens our connection to the universal energy that supports us.

The benefits of maintaining a consistent meditation practice extend beyond the immediate manifestation of our desires. It creates a ripple effect that permeates all aspects of our lives, leading to greater clarity, peace, and abundance. By making meditation a non-negotiable part of our daily routine, we pave the way for a life of limitless possibilities and ultimate manifestation.

Gratitude: Attracting Abundance Through Appreciation

Gratitude is a concept that has been praised by many as a powerful tool for attracting abundance into one's life. The idea is simple yet profound: by cultivating a grateful mindset, we open ourselves up to receiving more of what we desire. In this book, I will explore the connection between gratitude and manifestation, and how adopting a grateful mindset can transform our lives.

The importance of a grateful mindset in manifestation cannot be overstated. When we focus on what we lack or what is not going well in our lives, we are essentially putting out negative energy into the universe. This negative energy only attracts more of the same, perpetuating a cycle of scarcity and dissatisfaction. However, when we shift our focus to what we are grateful for, we send out positive vibrations that attract abundance and positive experiences.

To illustrate the power of gratitude, I will introduce you to a character who embarks on a journey of gratitude and abundance. This character, let's call them Alex, initially struggles with negative thoughts and a scarcity mindset. Alex feels like they never have enough and constantly compared themselves to others. They believe that they are not deserving of abundance and that they will never achieve their dreams.

However, everything changes when Alex starts to cultivate gratitude through daily practices. They begin keeping a gratitude journal, jotting down three things they are grateful for each day. They also make an effort to express appreciation to others, whether through a simple thank you or a heartfelt note. These small acts of gratitude start to shift Alex's perspective.

As Alex continues their journey, they start to notice the positive aspects of their life that they had previously overlooked. They find gratitude in even the smallest things, like the warmth of the sun on their face or the sound of birds chirping in the morning. These simple moments of appreciation bring a sense of joy and contentment that Alex had never experienced before.

With each day, Alex's mindset continues to shift. They focus less on what they lack and more on what they have. And as their focus shifts, so does their reality. Opportunities start to present themselves, seemingly out of nowhere. Alex receives unexpected gifts, financial opportunities arise, and their relationships improve. It becomes clear to Alex that their newfound mindset of gratitude is attracting abundance into their life.

Through specific examples, I will share how gratitude has brought abundance into Alex's life. These examples will serve as inspiration for readers, showing them that cultivating a grateful mindset can lead to tangible results. From financial windfalls to improved health, the power of gratitude knows no bounds.

Throughout this journey, Alex gains a deeper understanding of the connection between gratitude and abundance. They realize that gratitude is not just a one-time practice, but a way of life. It is a daily commitment to noticing and appreciating the good in our lives. This understanding fundamentally changes Alex's perspective on life, and they become a living testament to the power of gratitude in manifestation.

To help readers cultivate their own grateful mindset and attract abundance through gratitude, I will offer practical tips and exercises. From gratitude journaling to random acts of kindness, these practices will empower readers to shift their focus and open themselves up to the endless possibilities that come with a grateful mindset.

In the following chapters, I will delve deeper into the transformative power of gratitude. I will discuss the scientific research and studies that support the connection between gratitude and manifestation. I will also offer additional insights and perspectives on the role of appreciation in attracting abundance. Finally, I will encourage readers to continue practicing gratitude and remind them that this journey is ongoing, with new levels of abundance awaiting them as they continue to cultivate a grateful mindset.

Gratitude is the ultimate power of manifestation, and through this book, I hope to inspire and empower readers to unlock this power within themselves. So, let's embark on this journey together and discover the incredible abundance that awaits us through the practice of gratitude.

Journaling: Writing Your Way to Manifestation

Journaling has always been a powerful tool for self-reflection and personal growth. In the context of manifestation, it becomes an even more potent instrument for bringing our desires into reality. In this subchapter, we will explore the incredible power of journaling as a tool for manifestation and how it can help readers manifest their deepest desires.

Journaling allows us to delve into our thoughts, emotions, and desires, and brings them to the forefront of our consciousness. By writing down our thoughts and intentions, we give them a tangible form, making them more real and concrete. This act of writing helps us clarify our desires and set clear intentions, enabling us to focus our energy and attention on what truly matters.

When we journal, we create a safe space for self-reflection and exploration. We can dive deep into our desires and uncover what truly ignites our passion and purpose. By using journaling prompts, we can identify and articulate our desires with clarity and precision. The act of writing them down helps solidify our intentions and makes them more tangible. It is a powerful step towards manifesting our desires.

In addition to clarifying our desires, journaling also helps us release limiting beliefs and negative thought patterns. By writing down our fears and doubts, we bring them into the light and can examine them with objectivity. Journaling prompts can guide us to uncover and challenge our limiting beliefs, allowing us to rewrite our narratives and create new empowering stories. It is through this process that we can shed the weight of self-imposed limitations and move towards our desires with confidence and conviction.

To support manifestation, there are specific journaling exercises that can be highly effective. One such exercise is releasing limiting beliefs and negative thought patterns. By using prompts that encourage us to question and challenge our beliefs, we can begin to dismantle the barriers that hold us back from manifesting our desires. Visualization exercises and gratitude journaling are also powerful manifestation practices. By visualizing our desires and expressing gratitude for what we already have, we shift our focus towards abundance and attract more of what we desire into our lives.

Tracking progress is essential to stay motivated and aligned with our desires. Journaling provides a space for us to reflect on our manifestation journey and evaluate our progress. By setting measurable goals and regularly assessing our outcomes, we can make adjustments and course correct as needed. Journaling prompts that prompt us to track our progress can be invaluable in keeping us on track and accountable to ourselves.

The frequency of journaling for manifestation may vary for each individual. However, a regular practice is recommended to maintain consistency and momentum. Finding a journaling routine that works for you is crucial. Whether it's daily, weekly, or even monthly, carving out dedicated time for journaling ensures that you stay connected to your desires and remain focused on your manifestation journey.

To get the most out of manifestation journaling, there are a few tips to keep in mind. First and foremost, authenticity and honesty are key. Journaling is a personal and private practice, so it's important to be true to yourself and express your thoughts and emotions without judgment. Creating a safe and non-judgmental space for journaling is also vital. Find a quiet and peaceful environment where you can freely express yourself without fear of criticism or ridicule.

While journaling is a powerful tool for manifestation, it is important to note that it is not the sole means of manifesting our desires. Taking inspired action and aligning our thoughts, emotions, and actions are equally crucial. Journaling supports our manifestation journey by helping us clarify our desires, release limiting beliefs, and track our progress. However, it is through intentional action and alignment that we bring our desires into reality.

In conclusion, journaling is a transformative practice that can greatly enhance our manifestation journey. It allows us to clarify our desires, release limiting beliefs, and track our progress. By using the journaling prompts and exercises provided, we can tap into the power of manifestation and create the life we truly desire. So, grab your journal and get ready to manifest your deepest desires. The power is within you.

Creative Expression: Using Art and Creativity for Manifestation

Throughout history, art has been a powerful tool for self-expression and manifestation. It has allowed individuals to tap into their creative potential and bring their desires into reality. Art, in all its forms, has a unique ability to transcend language barriers and communicate on a deep, emotional level. In this book, I will explore the power of art as a tool for manifestation and delve into the connection between creativity and the manifestation process.

Understanding Manifestation:

Manifestation is the process of bringing our desires and intentions into reality. It is the understanding that our thoughts and beliefs create our reality. By harnessing the power of our minds, we have the ability to shape our lives and manifest our deepest desires. Creativity plays a crucial role in this process, as it allows us to tap into the unlimited potential of our imagination and bring forth our desires with intention.

Tapping into Creative Potential:

Every individual has a wellspring of creative potential within them, waiting to be tapped into. By exploring different techniques and exercises, we can unleash our creativity and unlock our true manifesting power. Whether it's through painting, writing, or music, there are countless ways to cultivate a creative mindset. By embracing our unique abilities and letting go of self-doubt, we can access our creative potential and manifest our desires.

Using Art as a Manifestation Tool:

Art has the remarkable ability to help us visualize our desires and bring them into reality. By engaging in artistic mediums such as painting, drawing, writing, or music, we can create tangible representations of our desires. Through the process of artistic expression, we are able to channel our intentions and connect deeply with our desires. Art becomes a powerful manifestation tool, bridging the gap between the inner world of our thoughts and the outer world of our reality.

Creating a Manifestation Art Piece:

Creating a manifestation art piece is a step-by-step process that allows us to set clear intentions and visualize our desired outcomes. By first setting our intentions and clarifying what we want to manifest, we can then visualize these desires as we embark on the creative journey. This can be done through various techniques and materials, such as sketching, collaging, or even writing down affirmations. The creation process itself becomes a powerful tool for manifestation.

The Power of Intention in Art:

Intention is a crucial element in both art and manifestation. By setting clear intentions, we enhance the manifestation process and align our creative energy with our desires. Infusing intention into our art can be done through affirmations, symbolism, or even the choice of colors and materials. When our intentions are consciously embedded into our artwork, they become a powerful magnet that attracts our desires into our reality.

Expressing Desires through Art:

Art provides a visual language through which we can express our desires. It allows us to represent our goals, dreams, and aspirations in a tangible and meaningful way. By visually representing our desires, we create a constant reminder and reinforcement of what we want to manifest. Art becomes a tool for focusing our energy and directing our attention towards our desired outcomes.

Using Creativity to Overcome Blocks:

Creativity has the transformative power to help us overcome blocks and limitations. The process of creating art can be cathartic and transformative, allowing us to release emotional barriers and tap into our subconscious mind. By delving into our creativity, we can access our true desires and manifest them with ease. Art becomes a gateway to our authentic selves and a powerful tool for personal growth and transformation.

Embracing the Journey of Creation:

In the process of creating art, it is important to embrace the journey rather than solely focusing on the end result. The act of creation itself brings joy, fulfillment, and growth. It allows us to explore new possibilities, challenge our limits, and expand our horizons. By embracing the journey of creation, we not only manifest our desires but also experience personal transformation and self-discovery.

Harnessing the Power of Art in Everyday Life:

Art has the potential to infuse our everyday lives with creativity and inspiration. By incorporating art into our daily routines, we can tap into our creative potential and manifest our desires consistently. Whether it's through journaling, doodling, or simply taking a moment to appreciate the beauty around us, art becomes a transformative practice that enhances our manifestation journey. Consistently practicing art and using it as a manifestation tool allows us to harness its power and create a life aligned with our deepest desires.

Chapter 6: The Transformative Power of Meditation

Exploring Different Meditation Techniques

When it comes to achieving overall well-being and personal growth, meditation plays a vital role. It is a practice that has been embraced by cultures all over the world for centuries, and its benefits are well-documented. In this subchapter, we will delve into the fascinating world of meditation, exploring various techniques and uncovering the incredible power they hold.

Meditation, at its core, is a state of deep focus and relaxation. Its historical roots can be traced back to ancient civilizations, where it was used as a means to achieve spiritual enlightenment. Today, meditation has evolved to encompass a wide range of practices, each with its own unique principles and goals. Whether it's reducing stress, increasing self-awareness, or improving focus, meditation has something to offer for everyone.

The benefits of meditation are wide-ranging and have been scientifically proven time and time again. From reducing stress and anxiety to improving mental clarity and focus, the positive effects of meditation on mental and physical health are well-documented. Countless studies have shown that regular meditation practice can lead to increased self-awareness, improved emotional well-being, and enhanced overall cognitive function. It's no wonder that meditation has become an integral part of many people's daily routines.

One of the most popular meditation techniques in recent years is mindfulness meditation. Originating from Buddhist traditions, mindfulness meditation has gained significant traction in Western societies. At its core, mindfulness meditation emphasizes present-moment awareness and non-judgmental acceptance of thoughts and emotions. By practicing mindfulness, individuals can reduce stress, improve emotional well-being, and cultivate a deeper sense of peace and contentment.

Loving-kindness meditation, also known as Metta meditation, is another powerful technique worth exploring. Rooted in Buddhist tradition, loving-kindness meditation focuses on cultivating feelings of compassion, love, and goodwill towards oneself and others. This practice has been found to increase empathy, reduce negative emotions, and foster a greater sense of connection and compassion towards oneself and the world at large.

Transcendental Meditation (TM) offers a unique approach to meditation, with origins in Hinduism. This technique involves the use of a silent mantra to achieve deep relaxation and self-awareness. By silently repeating a mantra, practitioners of TM are able to enter a state of profound calm and clarity. The benefits of transcendental meditation include improved focus, reduced anxiety, and an overall sense of inner peace and well-being.

For those who prefer a more active form of meditation, walking meditation provides a wonderful opportunity to combine mindfulness with movement. With its roots in Buddhist tradition, walking meditation places a strong emphasis on mindful walking and the integration of movement with breath and awareness. By engaging in this practice, individuals can improve their physical fitness, enhance their mind-body connection, and experience a sense of calm and roundedness.

Visualization meditation is another powerful technique that harnesses the power of mental imagery to promote relaxation and positive change. By creating vivid mental images and visualizing desired outcomes, individuals can enhance their creativity, set goals, and boost their self-confidence. The benefits of visualization meditation are vast and include increased motivation, improved performance, and a greater sense of self-belief.

Body scan meditation offers a unique approach to relaxation and self-care. With its focus on systematically scanning and releasing tension from different parts of the body, this technique promotes deep relaxation and body awareness. By practicing body scan meditation, individuals can reduce muscle tension, improve sleep quality, and cultivate a greater sense of overall well-being.

In conclusion, exploring different meditation techniques can be a transformative journey. By immersing ourselves in these practices, we open ourselves up to a world of profound benefits, from stress reduction to increased self-awareness and improved focus. I encourage you to experiment with different techniques and find the ones that resonate with your individual preferences and goals. The power of manifestation lies within you, waiting to be awakened through the practice of meditation.

Cultivating Mindfulness and Presence

In this section, I will delve into the subchapter "Cultivating Mindfulness and Presence" and its significance in establishing a deeper connection with the present moment through the practice of meditation. Through this exploration, we will uncover how meditation can elevate our levels of mindfulness and presence, ultimately leading to a more profound experience of the present moment.

Defining Terms:

Let us first establish a clear understanding of the terms we will be discussing. Mindfulness can be defined as the intentional act of paying attention to the present moment without judgment. It involves being fully present and engaged, without being distracted by thoughts or external stimuli. On the other hand, presence refers to the state of complete awareness and engagement in the current moment. When we cultivate mindfulness and presence, we invite a greater sense of clarity, calmness, and overall well-being into our lives.

Objectives and Scope:

In this subchapter, our primary goal is to equip you with techniques and exercises for developing mindfulness and presence through the practice of meditation. We will cover a range of topics, including different meditation techniques, the benefits of mindfulness and presence, and tips for incorporating these practices into your daily life.

Methodology and Approach:

Our approach in this subchapter will be grounded in research studies and expert opinions, highlighting the effectiveness of meditation in cultivating mindfulness and presence. We will draw upon various theoretical frameworks and models, such as the Mindfulness-Based Stress Reduction (MBSR) program and the teachings of renowned meditation teachers, to provide a comprehensive understanding of these practices.

Exploring Different Meditation Techniques:

Now, let us explore the various meditation techniques that can be used to cultivate mindfulness and presence. Focused attention meditation involves directing your attention to a specific object, such as your breath, and continuously bringing your focus back to it whenever your mind wanders. Loving-kindness meditation focuses on developing feelings of compassion and love towards yourself and others. Body scan meditation involves systematically scanning your body with your awareness, bringing attention to any sensations or areas of tension.

Each technique offers unique benefits and features. We will provide detailed instructions on how to practice each technique effectively, ensuring that you can fully engage in these practices and reap their rewards.

Developing Mindfulness in Daily Life:

Incorporating mindfulness into our daily activities is crucial for maintaining a present and engaged state of mind. We will share tips and strategies for infusing mindfulness into various aspects of your life, such as mindful eating, mindful walking, and mindful communication. By integrating these practices into your routine, you will find yourself more present and fully immersed in the richness of each experience.

Enhancing Presence through Meditation:

Through regular meditation practice, we can cultivate a deeper sense of presence by training our minds to let go of distractions and focus solely on the present moment. This heightened presence allows us to fully engage in various situations, enabling us to make the most of every opportunity. We will delve into how meditation can strengthen our ability to stay present and fully engaged, enhancing our overall experience of life.

The Power of Manifestation:

Now, let us explore how developing mindfulness and presence through meditation can enhance the power of manifestation. By being fully present and aware, we align our thoughts, beliefs, and actions with our desires, setting the stage for a more effective manifestation process. We will discuss the profound impact that mindfulness and presence can have on our ability to manifest our goals and dreams.

Techniques for Harnessing the Ultimate Power of Manifestation:

To harness the ultimate power of manifestation, we will introduce you to specific techniques and exercises that can be incorporated into your meditation sessions. These techniques include visualization, affirmation, and gratitude practices. By integrating these practices into your meditation routine, you can amplify their effectiveness and accelerate your manifestation journey.

Benefits and Conclusion:

Cultivating mindfulness and presence through meditation offers a myriad of benefits. Improved focus, reduced stress, and increased self-awareness are just a few of the transformative outcomes you can expect. As we conclude this subchapter, we emphasize the importance of regular practice and the potential for personal growth that awaits those who embark on this journey.

Using Meditation to Cultivate Inner Peace

Meditation has long been recognized as a powerful tool for cultivating inner peace and harmony. In today's fast-paced and often chaotic world, finding a sense of calm and centeredness is more important than ever. Through the practice of meditation, we can tap into the ultimate power of manifestation and create a peaceful state of mind that permeates every aspect of our lives.

Understanding Different Styles of Meditation:

There are various styles of meditation, each offering its unique approach to cultivating inner peace. Two popular styles are Open Presence (OP) and Focused Attention (FA). Open Presence meditation involves being fully present in the moment, without judgment, and allowing thoughts and sensations to come and go. It encourages a deep sense of acceptance and mindfulness. On the other hand, Focused Attention meditation involves focusing on a specific object or sensation, such as the breath. This style cultivates concentration and calmness. The key is to choose a style that resonates with you and aligns with your goals.

The Calming Effects of Meditation:

Research has shown that meditation has profound effects on reducing stress, anxiety, and negative emotions. By practicing meditation regularly, we can create a peaceful and harmonious internal environment. When negative states of mind decrease, we naturally experience a greater sense of peace and tranquility. Meditation has the potential to transform our internal landscape and create a positive ripple effect in our external world.

The Influence of Long-term Meditators:

Long-term meditators have been found to have a profound influence on those around them. Their presence alone can inspire others to cultivate a greater sense of well-being and happiness. Studies and anecdotes abound, highlighting the positive impact that meditators have on their environment. By radiating peace and harmony, they create a ripple effect that extends far beyond their personal practice. This ripple effect has the potential to transform communities and societies, fostering a more peaceful and harmonious world.

Exploring Tantric Wind Meditation:

Another style of meditation worth exploring is Tantric Wind meditation. This practice aims to shift energy flow in the body through visualizations and breath practices. By engaging with this unique style, we can further deepen our inner peace and harmony. Tantric Wind meditation offers a range of benefits, from increased energy flow to heightened awareness of the mind-body connection. Its incorporation into our meditation practice can enhance our ability to manifest peace and harmony in our daily lives.

State Changes During Meditation:

During meditation, we may experience various states, such as a cessation of internal dialogue, a deep sense of peace and calmness, and moments of perceptual clarity. These state changes contribute to the cultivation of inner peace and harmony. Meditation provides a sanctuary from the noise and chaos of everyday life, allowing us to tap into a deeper sense of tranquility. It is within these moments of stillness that we can truly connect with ourselves and manifest a more peaceful existence.

Lasting Effects of Meditation:

One of the most remarkable aspects of meditation is its ability to create lasting trait changes. Through regular practice, we can reshape our responses to stress and maintain a sense of peace and harmony beyond the meditation cushion. Numerous studies and personal experiences support the notion that meditation has lasting effects on our overall well-being. By incorporating meditation into our daily routine, we can create a life that is consistently peaceful and harmonious.

Practical Tips for Cultivating Inner Peace through Meditation:

For those seeking to cultivate inner peace and harmony through meditation, here are some practical tips. Firstly, take the time to find the meditation style that resonates with you. Experiment with different techniques and approaches until you find what feels right. Secondly, establish a consistent meditation practice. Carve out a dedicated space and time for meditation each day, even if it's just a few minutes. Consistency is key to reaping the full benefits of meditation. Lastly, consider incorporating additional resources or techniques that complement meditation and enhance its calming effects. This could include practices such as breathwork, journaling, or visualization exercises.

Exploring the Connection between Meditation and Inner Peace:

Beyond the physical and mental benefits, meditation offers a deeper connection to inner peace. Through this practice, we can align ourselves with our true selves and tap into a greater connection to the present moment. This profound connection enhances our ability to manifest peace and harmony in our lives. Meditation becomes a gateway to our true nature, a state of being that is inherently peaceful and harmonious.

Conclusion:

In conclusion, meditation is a powerful tool for cultivating inner peace and harmony. Through understanding different styles of meditation, exploring its calming effects, and observing the influence of long-term meditators, we can harness the ultimate power of manifestation. By exploring unique practices like Tantric Wind meditation, experiencing state changes during our practice, and recognizing the lasting effects of meditation, we can transform our lives into a more peaceful and harmonious existence. By incorporating practical tips and deepening our connection to meditation, we can manifest a life filled with inner peace and harmony. So, take the first step on this transformative journey and discover the ultimate power of meditation.

The Transformative Power of Meditation

The Science and Benefits of Meditation

Hey there!

Have you ever felt like life is constantly throwing stress your way? I know I have. It seems like in today's fast-paced world, stress has become anelcome companion, always tagging along and dampening our ability to manifest our desires. But fear not! There is a way to alleviate the burdens of stress and create a tranquil state of mind that is conducive to manifestation. And that way is through the regular practice of meditation.

Now, I know what you might be thinking - "Meditation? Isn't that just sitting still and doing nothing?" Well, yes and no. It's not just sitting still and twiddling our thumbs. It's about finding a quiet space, closing our eyes, and diving deep into the world within. Research has shown that meditation activates the relaxation response in our bodies, reducing the production of stress hormones and allowing our minds to be in a calmer state. And when our minds are calmer, we can focus more clearly on our intentions and attract our desires with greater precision.

But it's not just stress reduction that makes meditation a powerful tool for manifestation. It also enhances our focus and attention. Can you imagine how much easier it would be to visualize our desired reality and notice the signs and synchronicities that guide us towards our manifestations? Well, that's exactly what meditation can help us achieve. By sitting in stillness and quieting our minds, we improve our ability to concentrate on our desires and align our thoughts with our intentions. Scientific studies have even shown that regular meditation can lead to an increase in grey matter concentration in the brain regions associated with attention and emotional regulation. So, it's like giving our focus and manifestation abilities a little boost.

But wait, there's more! Meditation also has this incredible power to align our mind, body, and spirit. It allows us to tap into the immense power within ourselves. When we meditate, we dive into our subconscious mind - the gateway to our beliefs and emotions. And this is where the magic happens. By delving into our subconscious, we can identify and release any limiting beliefs that may be hindering our manifestation efforts. It's like pressing the reset button on our minds and consciously reprogramming them to align with the vibrations of abundance and success. Talk about a game-changer!

Now, I want to be real with you. The effects of meditation may not be immediate. Just like manifestation itself, it's a journey. It's about consistency and commitment. By incorporating meditation into our daily routine, we can gradually cultivate a state of mind that is receptive to the manifestation of our desires. Each session nourishes the connection between our mind, body, and spirit, allowing them to harmonize and work in unison towards the realization of our intentions. It's a process, but trust me, it's worth it.

So, my fellow manifestos, let's embrace the transformative power of meditation. Let's make it a cornerstone of our practice, delving into the unlimited potential that lies within us. By nurturing our inner world and cultivating a tranquil state of mind, we unlock the doorway to our dreams, inviting them to manifest with grace and ease. Are you ready to embark on this journey with me? Let's tap into our manifesting powers and create the life we've always dreamed of.

Have you ever felt a profound desire for something, but couldn't quite figure out how to bring it into your reality? That was me until I discovered the incredible power of manifestation meditation techniques. Let me take you on a journey through my personal experiences and show you how meditation became the key to unlocking the possibilities in my life.

Visualization became my secret weapon when it came to manifesting my desires. I would close my eyes, take deep breaths, and immerse myself in a vivid picture of the reality I wanted to create. Every detail, every sensation, became crystal clear in my mind. I could see myself in my dream job, surrounded by loving relationships, and living a life of abundance. The more I allowed myself to feel the emotions associated with these visions, the more I felt the universe responding and aligning with my intentions.

But manifestation goes deeper than just visualization. In the chaos of everyday life, it's easy to lose touch with our inner wisdom – the voice that guides us towards our true desires and purpose. Through meditation, I found a sacred space where I could connect with that inner wisdom. By quieting my mind and turning my attention inward, I could hear the whispers of my soul, telling me the steps I needed to take in my manifestation journey. It was through this connection with my inner wisdom that I found clarity and direction.

And then there's the universal energy that surrounds us, waiting to be tapped into. During my meditation practice, I would imagine myself as a vessel, open and receptive to the flow of this energy. I could feel it coursing through my body, filling me with a sense of empowerment and alignment. By consciously connecting with this universal energy, I could amplify my manifestations and bring them into reality with greater ease.

With each meditation session, I could feel myself getting closer to my dreams. It was as if the universe was conspiring to make them come true. It wasn't just about the techniques, though. It was about combining them with a dedicated mindset and unwavering belief in the power of manifestation. These techniques were merely tools to enhance the journey.

In the next chapter, I will share practical tools that have further enhanced my manifestation process. From vision boards to crystals to essential oils, these tools can serve as powerful allies in our quest for manifestation. But remember, it's the combination of these techniques with an open heart and a steadfast belief in our own power that truly unlocks the ultimate potential of manifestation. So, let's dive in and discover the magic that awaits us.

Creating a Sacred Space for Meditation

I remember when I first embarked on my journey of manifestation, I quickly discovered the incredible importance of having a sacred space for meditation. This space would be my sanctuary, a place where I could escape from the chaos of the outside world and truly connect with my inner self. And let me tell you, it was a game-changer.

In this chapter, I want to guide you through the process of creating your very own sacred space. Trust me, it's worth it. This space will enhance your meditation experience and allow you to tap into the infinite power of manifestation. Are you ready?

Step 1: Setting Up an Altar

Ah, the altar. This is where the magic happens. It's your dedicated space, the focal point of your practice. And guess what? It can be as simple or as elaborate as you want it to be. Find a surface, like a table or a shelf, that feels peaceful and allows you to practice without any interruptions.

Now, gather meaningful objects that speak to your soul. Maybe it's a statue that represents your spiritual beliefs, or a symbol that holds special meaning for you. You can even include personal mementos, like photographs of loved ones or cherished items. Arrange them on your altar in a way that feels harmonious and inspiring to you.

Step 2: Utilizing Essential Oils and Candles

Ah, the power of scent and flickering light. Essential oils and candles are like the perfect duet, creating a serene and relaxing atmosphere for your meditation practice. Choose scents that promote tranquility, such as lavender, chamomile, or sandalwood. And hey, feel free to mix and match!

Place a few drops of your chosen essential oil in a diffuser, and let it fill the air with its calming aroma. Ahh, can you already feel yourself drifting into a state of deep relaxation?

Now, let's talk about candles. They bring a warm and gentle glow that helps you focus your attention. opt for unscented candles or ones that complement your chosen essential oil. As you light the candles before your meditation session, let their soft light guide you into a state of peace.

Step 3: Incorporating Crystals

Crystals, my friend, hold incredible power. They can amplify energy and promote deep spiritual connection. And lucky for you, they're perfect for your sacred space! Choose crystals that resonate with you and your journey. Some great ones for manifestation include clear quartz, amethyst, and citrine.

Now, strategically place these crystals around your sacred space. You can make a large crystal the centerpiece of your altar, surrounded by smaller crystals. Or if you prefer, hold a crystal in your hand during meditation to amplify its magic.

Step 4: Personalization

Now, here's the best part. Your sacred space should be all about you. It should reflect your unique journey, your preferences, and your spirit. So, let your creative juices flow! Add artwork, plants, or objects that hold significant meaning to your spiritual practice.

Embrace this opportunity to create a space that truly resonates with you. When you step into this sacred space, you'll feel an undeniable connection to the universe and your own inner self. This connection will elevate your meditation practice and, trust me, your ability to manifest your desires.

Incorporating these techniques into your sacred space for meditation will cultivate an environment of peace, tranquility, and deep spiritual connection. As you enter this space, leave behind the distractions of the outside world and enter a realm of endless possibilities. Embrace this practice wholeheartedly, my friend, and watch as your manifestation journey reaches new heights.

Now, go create your sacred space! The universe is waiting.

Chapter 7: The Power of Journaling

Manifestation Journaling Prompts

Manifestation is a concept that has gained significant popularity in recent years, particularly in the realm of personal development and goal achievement. It is the idea that we have the power to attract and create the life we desire through our thoughts, beliefs, and actions. In my book, "Manifestation: The Ultimate Power of Manifestation," I delve into the various aspects of manifestation and provide practical tools and techniques to harness this power.

One of the key tools I discuss in the book is journaling. Journaling serves as a powerful tool for self-reflection and exploration of desires and beliefs. By putting our thoughts and feelings onto paper, we gain clarity and insights into our deepest desires and aspirations. It allows us to uncover what truly drives us and what we want to manifest in our lives.

To kickstart the journaling process, I introduce the first journaling prompt: "What are your deepest desires and aspirations?" This prompt encourages readers to dig deep and explore their personal dreams, goals, and aspirations. It is an invitation to connect with the innermost desires that often get buried under the weight of societal expectations and limiting beliefs.

Identifying and addressing limiting beliefs is another crucial step in the manifestation process. Limiting beliefs are the negative thoughts and beliefs we hold about ourselves and our ability to manifest. These beliefs often stem from past experiences, societal conditioning, and fear of failure. In my book, I guide readers to recognize and challenge these limiting beliefs through the second journaling prompt: "What limiting beliefs do you hold about yourself and your ability to manifest?"

Reframing these limiting beliefs into empowering beliefs is a powerful practice that enables us to shift our mindset and align it with our desires. By consciously choosing empowering beliefs, we open ourselves up to new possibilities and opportunities. The third journaling prompt, "How can you reframe those limiting beliefs into empowering beliefs?" guides readers through the process of reframing beliefs. I provide examples and techniques, such as affirmations and positive self-talk, to help readers rewrite their internal narratives and cultivate a mindset of abundance and possibility.

Setting specific manifestation goals is essential for focus and clarity. In my book, I emphasize the importance of defining and clarifying desired manifestations. The fourth journaling prompt, "What specific manifestations do you want to focus on?" encourages readers to get specific about what they want to manifest in different areas of their lives. By setting clear intentions, we create a roadmap that guides our thoughts, emotions, and actions towards our desired manifestations.

Aligning thoughts, emotions, and actions with our desired manifestations is crucial for bringing them into reality. In the book, I explain the importance of this alignment and provide strategies and exercises to cultivate it. The fifth journaling prompt, "How can you align your thoughts, emotions, and actions with your desired manifestations?" invites readers to explore ways in which they can align their inner and outer worlds to support their manifestations.

To strengthen manifestation abilities, I introduce the concept of daily manifestation practices. These practices serve as a consistent reminder and reinforcement of our desires and beliefs. The sixth journaling prompt, "What daily practices can you incorporate to strengthen your manifestation abilities?" encourages readers to explore various practices, such as gratitude journaling, visualization, and meditation, that can help them cultivate a strong manifestation mindset.

Cultivating a mindset of gratitude and abundance is a powerful practice that enhances the manifestation process. In my book, I highlight the benefits of cultivating this mindset and provide tips and exercises to develop a gratitude practice and shift our mindset towards abundance. The seventh journaling prompt, "How can you cultivate a mindset of gratitude and abundance?" invites readers to explore ways in which they can foster a sense of gratitude and abundance in their daily lives.

Releasing resistance and surrendering to the flow of manifestation is another key aspect I address in the book. Resistance often arises from our attachment to specific outcomes and our fear of the unknown. In order to allow manifestation to unfold naturally, we must learn to release resistance and surrender control. The eighth journaling prompt, "What steps can you take to release resistance and surrender to the flow of manifestation?" offers readers techniques and guidance to let go of resistance and embrace the process of manifestation.

Visualization and affirmations are powerful tools that amplify our manifestations. By vividly imagining our desired outcomes and affirming them with conviction, we create a strong energetic connection with our desires. In the book, I explain the power of visualization and affirmations and provide exercises and examples for incorporating them into our daily journaling practice. The ninth journaling prompt, "How can you use visualization and affirmations to amplify your manifestations?" encourages readers to explore creative ways in which they can leverage these tools to enhance their manifestation practice.

By following the structure and utilizing these journaling prompts, readers can embark on a transformative journey of self-discovery and manifestation. Through reflection, reframing, and realignment, they can tap into their ultimate power to manifest the life they truly desire.

Scripting Your Ideal Reality

As I sit here with my journal and pen in hand, I am filled with excitement and anticipation. Today, I am going to introduce you to the incredible power of scripting your ideal reality through journaling. This practice, when combined with the power of visualization, has the ability to manifest your deepest desires.

Visualizing is more than just daydreaming; it is the act of vividly imagining yourself in the reality you wish to create. When you combine this with the written word, through scripting, you create a powerful tool for manifestation. By detailing your desires in writing, you are sending a clear message to the universe about what you want to bring into your life.

One of the key elements in scripting your ideal reality is the importance of turning point memories. These memories serve as anchor points for your scripting and visualization exercises. They are moments in your life where everything changed, where you experienced a profound shift in perspective or had an epiphany. These turning points have the potential to shape your future and align you with your desires.

Before these turning points, we often find ourselves in challenging situations, with negative beliefs or limiting mindsets holding us back. It is important to acknowledge and explore these aspects of our lives before we can fully appreciate the power of the turning point memory.

Now, let me take you back to my own turning point memory. It was a sunny afternoon, and I was feeling lost and unfulfilled in my career. Suddenly, a series of events unfolded that led me to a life-changing realization. I vividly remember the emotions, actions, and reactions I experienced in that moment. It was like a light bulb switched on in my mind, and I could see a new path before me.

This turning point memory served as a catalyst for positive change and manifestation in my life. It was the starting point for my transformation. It was through this experience that I truly understood the power of affirmations. Affirmations are positive statements that reprogram the subconscious mind and align us with our desires. By repeating affirmations daily, we can shift our beliefs and manifest our ideal reality.

One powerful method that incorporates affirmations is the 369 Manifestation Method. This technique involves repeating affirmations in the morning, afternoon, and evening. By consistently affirming our desires throughout the day, we create a strong energetic imprint that aligns us with our intentions.

To fully harness the power of manifestation, it is essential to understand the laws of attraction. There are different layers and categories within this universal law, and by understanding them, we can enhance our manifestation abilities. This knowledge allows us to align our thoughts, emotions, and actions with our desires, amplifying our ability to manifest.

Immersion is key in the process of manifesting. Consistent journaling, visualization, and scripting keep our desires at the forefront of our minds and maintain our focus. By immersing ourselves in these practices, we send a clear message to the universe about what we want to bring into our lives.

In conclusion, scripting your ideal reality is a powerful practice that can transform your life. By combining visualization, turning point memories, affirmations, and the 369 Manifestation Method, you have the ability to manifest your deepest desires. It is time to take action and start journaling, scripting, and visualizing your ideal reality. Your dreams are within reach, and it is up to you to make them a reality.

Reflective Journaling for Transformation

Reflective journaling has been a powerful tool in my own personal growth journey. It has allowed me to delve deep into my thoughts, emotions, and desires, ultimately leading to the manifestation of my dreams. Reflective journaling is a practice of self-reflection, where one can explore their innermost thoughts and gain clarity on their goals and aspirations.

Journaling has a transformative power that cannot be underestimated. By putting pen to paper, we are able to express ourselves in a way that we may not be able to verbally. It provides a safe space for self-expression, allowing us to release any pent-up emotions or thoughts. In turn, this enhances self-awareness and promotes personal growth. It is through this process of self-reflection that we are able to identify areas in our lives that may need improvement and take actionable steps towards positive change.

Keeping a journal has numerous benefits that extend beyond self-expression. It serves as a powerful tool for gaining clarity. By writing down our goals and desires, we are able to clarify our intentions and align our actions with our aspirations. Journaling also allows us to process our emotions and explore our thoughts and beliefs. Through this process, we can uncover any limiting beliefs or negative thought patterns that may be hindering our progress.

In addition to self-reflection, journaling provides a tangible record of our accomplishments, discoveries, and healings. By documenting these experiences, we are able to boost our confidence and foster a sense of achievement. It also serves as a reminder of our progress, especially during times when we may feel discouraged or stuck. This record of growth can be incredibly empowering and motivating.

Practicing gratitude is another essential component of journaling for transformation. By writing down at least twenty things that we are grateful for, we shift our mindset towards positivity and cultivate a sense of abundance. Gratitude has the power to attract more blessings into our lives and enhance our overall well-being. It is through this practice of gratitude that we begin to notice the synchronicities and miracles that are occurring in our lives.

Consistency is key when it comes to journaling. Making it a part of our daily routine creates a sense of discipline, commitment, and accountability. It is through regular journaling that we can truly experience long-term transformation and manifestation. This daily practice allows us to stay focused on our goals and take intentional action towards them.

Of course, no journey is without its challenges and obstacles. In journaling, we may encounter moments of resistance or self-doubt. However, by setting realistic goals, establishing a supportive environment, and seeking inspiration from others, we can overcome these challenges and continue on our path of growth.

There are various journaling techniques that can enhance the reflective process. From free writing to guided prompts to visual journaling, these techniques cater to individual preferences and enhance the overall journaling experience. It is important to explore these different techniques and find what resonates with us on a deeper level.

Ultimately, creating a personalized journaling practice is crucial. We must align our journaling practice with our unique needs, interests, and goals. By experimenting with different approaches, styles, and formats, we can find what works best for us. This personalized practice will ensure that our journaling journey is authentic and tailored to our individual growth and manifestation goals.

In conclusion, reflective journaling is a powerful tool for self-reflection, growth, and manifestation. By committing to a daily practice, we can unlock our true potential and manifest our dreams into reality. Through consistency, gratitude, and a personalized approach, we can tap into the ultimate power of manifestation and transform our lives.

Chapter 8: The Power of Creative Expression

Vision Board Collage

I first stumbled upon the concept of creating a vision board collage while reading a self-help book a few years ago. It immediately struck me as a fascinating tool for manifesting what one wants in life. Since then, I've noticed its popularity has grown exponentially, with many people using this visual representation of their desires to bring about positive change.

The process of creating a vision board collage is simple yet powerful. It involves cutting out photos and inspiring words from magazines or printing out online images that resonate with what one wants to attract into their life. These images are then arranged on a poster board and hung on the wall, where they are easily visible on a daily basis.

But what is the purpose of a vision board collage? It goes beyond just being a collection of pretty pictures. Its true purpose is to seed the subconscious mind with the desired images and activate the Law of Attraction. By having visual cues and reminders of what one wants, it helps generate thoughts about the desired outcome, creating a powerful magnet for manifestation.

One of the most intriguing aspects of creating a vision board collage is how it helps define and clarify what one wants to attract. The process of selecting images forces individuals to be specific and intentional about their desires and intentions. It's like creating a blueprint for the life one wants to create, giving it shape and form.

But a vision board collage goes even deeper. It serves as a map to the dissenting parts of oneself that may resist or doubt the desired outcomes. By having visual representations of what one wants, it becomes easier to identify and address any internal conflicts that may be holding one back. It allows for a deeper exploration of one's desires and the potential obstacles that may arise.

Now, it's important to note that a vision board collage should not be seen as having magical powers. It is simply a tool to focus on each image and give attention and love to one's vision. The Law of Attraction responds to what one gives the most attention and energy to. By focusing on a thought or image, it becomes more prominent in one's awareness and attracts matching experiences.

Consistency is key when it comes to using a vision board collage. Spending a few minutes every day focusing on what one wants can greatly increase the likelihood of attracting the desired experience. It's about creating a resonance with one's desires and aligning oneself with the energy of manifestation.

The benefits of having a vision board collage are numerous. It increases motivation, clarity, and inspiration. Regularly seeing the visual representation of one's desires keeps them at the forefront of the mind, serving as a constant reminder of what one is working towards.

Of course, there may be challenges or obstacles that arise when creating and using a vision board collage. Skepticism or doubts may creep in, causing individuals to question the effectiveness of this tool. However, I want to reassure and encourage you to embrace the power of visualization. Give it a try and see how it can transform your life.

In conclusion, actively engaging with a vision board collage is crucial. Revisit it regularly, make adjustments as necessary, and take inspired action towards your desires. Trust in the power of manifestation and the Law of Attraction. Create your own vision board collage and experience the transformative power of visualization in manifesting your desires.

Manifestation Art Journaling

Manifestation Art Journaling is a powerful practice that combines art and journaling for self-exploration and manifestation. It allows individuals to tap into their creative expression while also delving into their inner thoughts and desires. By using art as a form of communication with the subconscious mind, and journaling as a structured framework for setting intentions, manifestation art journaling offers a unique and effective way to explore one's desires and manifest them into reality.

The origins of manifestation art journaling can be traced back to ancient civilizations, where art and writing were used as tools for self-reflection and manifestation. Throughout history, this practice has evolved and gained popularity, with many influential figures in the manifestation art journaling community contributing to its growth. These key figures have shared their own experiences and techniques, inspiring others to embark on their own manifestation art journaling journeys.

Various techniques are used in manifestation art journaling, such as visualization, affirmation writing, and collage. Visualization allows individuals to create a vivid mental image of their desires, while affirmation writing helps to reinforce positive beliefs and intentions. Collage involves cutting and pasting images or words from magazines to create a visual representation of one's desires. These techniques, combined with the use of tools and materials such as paints, markers, and magazines, provide a multi-dimensional approach to manifestation art journaling.

The psychological and emotional benefits of manifestation art journaling are immense. Through this practice, individuals can gain clarity, set goals, and manifest their desires. Scientific research and studies have shown that manifestation art journaling can enhance overall well-being and increase feelings of empowerment. By engaging in this creative process, individuals can tap into their subconscious mind and access deeper emotions, allowing for a more holistic approach to self-discovery and manifestation.

Art and journaling work together harmoniously in the manifestation art journaling process. Art allows individuals to express their thoughts and emotions visually, while journaling provides a structured framework for setting intentions and documenting progress. By combining these two practices, individuals can effectively explore their desires, identify any blocks or limiting beliefs, and create a clear vision of what they want to manifest.

Manifestation art journaling serves as a powerful tool for manifestation. By using art and journaling to align their energy with their goals, individuals can create a clear path towards their desires. Techniques such as scripting or gratitude journaling can be incorporated into the art journaling process, further enhancing the manifestation experience.

Real-life examples and case studies showcase the effectiveness of manifestation art journaling. These stories highlight how individuals have used this practice to manifest their desires and achieve their goals. Common themes and strategies observed in successful manifestation art journaling experiences include consistency, belief in the process, and a willingness to explore and confront personal blocks or limiting beliefs.

Challenges and roadblocks are inevitable when practicing manifestation art journaling. However, by practicing self-reflection, shifting mindset, and seeking support from a community, individuals can overcome these challenges and continue on their manifestation journey. It is through perseverance and consistent practice that breakthroughs in manifestation can occur.

In conclusion, manifestation art journaling is a transformative practice that combines art and journaling for self-exploration and manifestation. By exploring desires, setting intentions, and aligning energy through art and journaling, individuals can manifest their desires and achieve their goals. Starting a manifestation art journaling practice can be a powerful step towards creating the life one desires. Additional resources and further steps can be taken to deepen understanding and practice of manifestation art journaling, allowing for continuous growth and manifestation.

Creative Visualization Techniques

In this subchapter, I want to introduce you to the incredible world of creative visualization techniques. These techniques go beyond simply visualizing your desires in your mind; they involve engaging in the artistic process of drawing, painting, and sculpting. By using these visual mediums, you can tap into the power of manifestation and bring your desires into reality.

When you use visual mediums to create a clear and detailed image of your desires, you are able to fully immerse yourself in the manifestation process. The clarity that comes from drawing, painting, and sculpting helps to solidify your intentions and make them more tangible. For example, if your desire is to travel to a specific destination, drawing or painting a picture of that place can help you visualize it with greater precision and detail.

Engaging in creative activities not only brings your desires into physical form, but it also makes them feel more real and achievable. By using drawing, painting, and sculpting, you are able to interact with your desires in a tangible way. For instance, if your desire is to have a successful business, creating a sculpture or painting related to your business can help you feel a deeper connection to your goal.

The act of drawing, painting, and sculpting taps into the power of imagination. Through these creative processes, you are able to visualize your desires with greater clarity and detail. By using your imagination in this way, you can enhance the visualization process and make it even more effective. For example, if your desire is to find true love, drawing or painting a picture of your ideal partner can help you imagine what they would look like and how they would make you feel.

One of the key benefits of using creative visualization techniques is the ability to focus your attention and energy. By engaging in drawing, painting, and sculpting, you are able to direct your energy towards your desires. This focused energy increases the likelihood of your desires coming into fruition. For instance, if your desire is to achieve financial abundance, creating a visual representation of your financial goals can help you stay focused and motivated.

Engaging in creative visualization techniques brings joy and fulfillment to the manifestation process. By using drawing, painting, and sculpting, you are able to express yourself creatively and find joy in the act of bringing your desires into reality. This joy and fulfillment enhance the manifestation process and make it even more powerful. For example, if your desire is to write a bestselling book, engaging in the creative process of painting or sculpting can help you tap into your creativity and bring joy to your writing journey.

Approaching creative visualization techniques with love, patience, and humility is crucial for mastering these techniques. These qualities allow you to approach your artistic endeavors with an open mind and a willingness to learn and grow. By applying these qualities to drawing, painting, and sculpting, you can develop a deeper connection with your desires and make them come to life. For example, approaching the act of painting with love and patience can help you create a masterpiece that represents your desired outcome.

Using creative visualization techniques harnesses the power of the Law of Attraction. The Law of Attraction states that like attracts like, and by focusing on positive thoughts and desires, you can attract them into your life. By using drawing, painting, and sculpting as tools for manifestation, you can tap into this universal law and align your energy with your desires. For example, if your desire is to become a successful entrepreneur, creating art that represents your entrepreneurial journey can help you attract the right opportunities and resources.

The benefits and rewards of using creative visualization techniques are vast. By practicing these techniques, you can bring fulfillment and success into your life. Many people have achieved their desires through the power of drawing, painting, and sculpting. For example, artists who visualize their desired outcomes through their art often find success and recognition in their creative careers.

In summary, creative visualization techniques are a powerful tool for manifestation. By engaging in drawing, painting, and sculpting, you can tap into your imagination, focus your energy, and bring joy and fulfillment to the manifestation process. I encourage you to explore and practice these techniques in your own life, as they have the potential to transform your desires into reality.

Chapter 9: The Art of Affirmations

Understanding the Science of Affirmations

Affirmations are the ultimate tool for rewiring the brain and shaping one's reality. They are powerful declarations that have the ability to attract or transform desired outcomes. By harnessing the power of affirmations, individuals can tap into the immense potential of their subconscious mind and create the life they truly desire.

The Power of Affirmations:

Affirmations work by declaring to oneself and the universe that the desired outcome is already created. They serve as a powerful reminder of the goals and dreams one is working towards. Through repetition, affirmations reinforce beliefs and help manifest desires. It is through the consistent and intentional use of affirmations that one can truly harness their power and create lasting change.

Creating Effective Affirmations:

Creating affirmations with power and faith is of utmost importance. It is essential to formulate affirmations in a way that omits any words that tie one to what they do not want. By focusing on what is desired, the subconscious mind is directed towards manifesting those desires. Affirmations should be crafted with intention and positivity, ensuring that every word aligns with the desired outcome.

Harnessing the Power of Feeling:

Adding feeling to affirmations is like adding fuel to a fire. It generates internal energy and amplifies the power of desires. Feeling is a key component in manifesting desired outcomes, as it creates a vibrational match with what is being affirmed. By truly embodying the emotions associated with the desired outcome, one becomes a magnet for its manifestation.

Addressing Stuck Emotional Energetic Patterns:

Stuck emotional energetic patterns can hinder the effectiveness of affirmations. These patterns are often deep-rooted and can prevent the subconscious mind from fully embracing and manifesting desires. Techniques such as emotional release exercises, meditation, and energy healing can be employed to shift these patterns and allow for more effective manifestation.

The Science Behind Affirmations:

Scientific research supports the effectiveness of affirmations in rewiring the brain. They have the power to reshape neural pathways and create new patterns of thinking. This phenomenon is known as neuroplasticity, which refers to the brain's ability to reorganize itself based on experiences and thoughts. By consistently practicing affirmations, individuals can create new neural connections and reinforce positive beliefs.

Neuroplasticity and Affirmations:

Neuroplasticity plays a crucial role in rewiring the brain through affirmations. By repeating affirmations and engaging in positive self-talk, individuals can strengthen the neural connections associated with their desires. This process leads to a shift in mindset and behavior, ultimately paving the way for the manifestation of desired outcomes.

Rewiring the Brain for Desired Outcomes:

Affirmations can be used as a powerful tool to rewire the brain for specific desired outcomes. Through consistent practice and repetition, affirmations create new neural pathways that support the manifestation of these desires. By rewiring the brain, individuals can align their thoughts, beliefs, and behaviors with their goals, leading to lasting changes and transformation.

The Role of Faith and Belief:

Faith and belief play a pivotal role in the effectiveness of affirmations. Having unwavering faith in the process and belief in the desired outcome enhances the power of affirmations. Doubt and skepticism can hinder manifestation, while faith and belief fuel the subconscious mind's ability to create the desired reality. It is through a strong foundation of faith and belief that affirmations become truly transformative.

Applying the Science of Affirmations to Shape Your Reality:

Understanding the science of affirmations empowers individuals to shape their own reality. By incorporating affirmations into daily life, one can consciously direct their thoughts and beliefs towards their desired outcomes. It is through consistent practice, intention, and belief that the power of affirmations is fully realized. With the practical steps and strategies outlined in this book, individuals can embark on a journey of positive transformation and manifest the life they truly desire.

Crafting effective affirmations is a powerful tool in harnessing the ultimate power of manifestation. The subconscious mind plays a crucial role in manifesting our desires, and affirmations serve as a bridge to communicate with this powerful aspect of our being. By understanding and utilizing affirmations effectively, we can unlock the hidden potential within us and manifest our dreams into reality.

Research Point 1 - Immersion is the Key to Mastery:

To truly master the art of manifestation, one must immerse themselves in the study of the law of attraction. This involves a diligent and dedicated exploration of its different components. By understanding the principles and mechanics behind the law of attraction, we can effectively align ourselves with its workings and manifest our desires more effortlessly. Immersion in this study allows us to gain a deeper understanding of the nuances and intricacies involved in the manifestation process.

Research Point 2 - Uncovering the Layers of the Law of Attraction:

The law of attraction is not a singular concept but rather a complex web of interconnected layers. To achieve greater success in manifestation, we must delve into these layers and master each category within the law of attraction. Whether it be the power of visualization, the influence of belief systems, or the impact of emotions, each layer offers its own unique insights and techniques for amplifying manifestation. By uncovering and mastering these layers, we unlock the full potential of manifestation.

Using Affirmations Effectively:

Affirmations serve as declarations of what is already present in our lives. By declaring our desires as if they are already created, we send a powerful message to the universe. The repetition of affirmations is crucial in programming the subconscious mind to manifest our desired reality. This repetition reinforces the belief that our desires are already within our reach, thus aligning our thoughts and emotions with the manifestation process.

Guidelines for Crafting Effective Affirmations:

Crafting effective affirmations requires clarity, positivity, and a sense of already having what we desire. It is important to use positive language and avoid statements of doubt or negativity. By stating our desires in the present tense and with clarity, we create a strong and clear intention that the universe can respond to. Our affirmations should be a reflection of our desires already being manifested.

The Universe is Always Listening:

It is crucial to understand that the universe is constantly listening and responding to our thoughts and affirmations. Every thought and affirmation emit energy and vibrations that the universe picks up on. Therefore, it is essential to align our thoughts with our desires, ensuring that our energy and vibrations are in harmony with what we wish to manifest. By aligning our thoughts with our desires, we create a powerful force that attracts what we seek.

Manifestation as a Tool for Personal Growth:

Manifestation is not limited to attracting material things; it is also a powerful tool for personal growth and transformation. Through the manifestation process, we can become the best version of ourselves, aligning with our true purpose and potential. By focusing on personal transformation, we attract not only the external manifestations we desire but also the internal growth and fulfillment that leads to a more fulfilling life.

The Law of Attraction and the Power of Positive Energy:

The law of attraction does not understand words like "don't, not, or no." It responds to the energy and vibrations we emit, which are influenced by our thoughts and emotions. It is therefore crucial to focus on what is desired rather than what is not desired. By harnessing positive energy and vibrations, we align ourselves with the desired outcome and attract more of what we want into our lives.

Living in the Present Moment for Manifestation:

Living in the present moment is essential for manifestation. It requires letting go of past regrets and future worries and fully immersing ourselves in the now. By focusing on the present moment, we align our thoughts, emotions, and actions with what we desire, creating a powerful force for manifestation. Letting go of attachment to outcomes and trusting the process allows the universe to work its magic in bringing our desires to fruition.

Fueling the Engine of Attraction through Action:

Aligning our thoughts and emotions with our desires is essential, but it is equally important to take inspired action. By aligning our thoughts, emotions, and actions, we create a powerful synergy that propels us towards our desired outcome. Positive thinking alone is not enough; we must also take tangible steps towards our goals. Through inspired action, we fuel the engine of attraction and bring our desires into reality.

The Secret of Surrender:

Surrendering to the universe and trusting the process is a fundamental aspect of manifestation. Letting go of attachment to outcomes and surrendering control allows the universe to work its magic in its own divine timing. By trusting that what is meant for us will come, we release resistance and open ourselves up to receiving our desires in the most perfect and effortless way.

Living the Law of Attraction as a Way of Life:

To truly harness the power of manifestation, we must integrate the principles of the law of attraction into every aspect of our lives. Consistently aligning our thoughts, emotions, and actions with our desires creates a state of constant manifestation. Trusting in the process and believing in our own power to create our reality is essential in living the law of attraction as a way of life. It is through this consistent alignment that we truly manifest our desires and live a life of abundance and fulfillment.

Integrating Affirmations into Daily Life

Incorporating affirmations into daily life is a concept that has gained significant popularity in the realm of self-help. Many individuals have found success and transformation by integrating affirmations into their routines. The power of affirmations lies in their ability to shift our mindset and focus, ultimately leading us towards the manifestation of our desires. In this chapter, I want to highlight the importance of practical strategies for making affirmations a seamless part of our daily lives.

To emphasize the practicality of affirmations, I would like to share a personal story or experience of someone who has successfully integrated affirmations into their daily routine. Let's call this person Sarah. Sarah, like many others, faced challenges in various aspects of her life. She struggled with self-doubt, lack of confidence, and a constant feeling of being stuck. However, once she started practicing affirmations regularly, she witnessed a profound change within herself.

Sarah's journey with affirmations was not without its obstacles. Initially, she found it difficult to truly believe in the power of affirmations. It took time and persistence to overcome her skepticism and doubts. Through consistent practice, Sarah began to experience positive changes in her life. She noticed a boost in her self-confidence, a newfound belief in her abilities, and a sense of empowerment that she had never felt before.

The impact of affirmations on Sarah's life was truly transformative. By aligning her thoughts and intentions with her desires, she was able to manifest incredible opportunities and experiences. Sarah's story serves as a testament to the power of affirmations and the immense potential they hold.

Now, let's delve into the first practical strategy for incorporating affirmations into our lives: becoming clear about what we want. Clarity is crucial when it comes to using affirmations effectively. Without a clear understanding of our desires and goals, affirmations can become vague and ineffective. To gain clarity, it is important to reflect on our deepest desires and aspirations. What do we truly want? What are our passions and dreams? By asking ourselves these questions and exploring our desires, we can begin to shape our affirmations in a way that resonates with our truest selves.

Once we have gained clarity about our desires, the next step is to write clear, positive affirmations. This is where the power of language comes into play. Affirmations should be written in the first person and present tense. By doing so, we tap into the power of the subconscious mind, which responds best to affirmations that are framed as present realities. It is also important to avoid using phrases like "I wish" or "someday," as they imply a lack of belief or doubt in the manifestation process. Instead, we should focus on writing affirmations that are concise, positive, and aligned with our desires.

Let me provide you with a few examples of clear, positive affirmations that can be used in daily practice:

"I am attracting abundance and prosperity into my life effortlessly."

"I am confident, capable, and worthy of success in all areas of my life."

"I am surrounded by love, joy, and positive energy."

"I am in perfect health and my body radiates vitality."

By incorporating these affirmations into our daily routine, we begin to shift our mindset and create a positive focus on our desires. This leads us to the next practical strategy: incorporating affirmations into our daily routine.

Repeating affirmations regularly throughout the day is key to their effectiveness. By seamlessly integrating affirmations into our daily activities, we ensure that they become an intrinsic part of our mindset and belief system. Simple practices such as reciting affirmations during our morning routine, writing them down and placing them in visible areas, or even using them as mantras during meditation can significantly enhance the impact of affirmations on our lives.

The benefits of making affirmations a consistent part of our routine is vast. Not only do they help us maintain a positive mindset, but they also serve as a constant reminder of our desires. Affirmations act as a guiding force, steering us towards our goals and aspirations. By incorporating them into our daily routine, we cultivate a sense of focus and determination that propels us towards the manifestation of our desires.

Shifting our mindset and maintaining a positive focus are crucial aspects of utilizing affirmations effectively. Affirmations have the power to transform our thoughts, which in turn shape our reality. By constantly reinforcing positive beliefs and intentions, we can overcome self-limiting beliefs and stay motivated towards our goals. Affirmations act as a beacon of light, guiding us through the ups and downs of our journey towards manifestation.

In order to fully understand the power of affirmations, it is essential to delve into the laws of attraction. The laws of attraction provide the framework through which affirmations work. By immersing ourselves in studying and learning about the laws of attraction, we gain a deeper understanding of how our thoughts and intentions shape our reality. The more we align our beliefs and actions with the principles of the laws of attraction, the more powerful our affirmations become.

For those seeking further study on the subject, I highly recommend resources such as "The Secret" by Rhonda Byrne, "Think and Grow Rich" by Napoleon Hill, and "The Power of Now" by Eckhart Tolle. These books offer valuable insights into the laws of attraction and provide practical strategies for incorporating affirmations into our lives.

Now, let's dive into the different layers and categories within the law of attraction. Understanding these layers is crucial for utilizing affirmations effectively. Each layer offers unique insights and techniques that can amplify the manifestation process. By mastering each part, we gain a comprehensive understanding of the law of attraction and enhance our ability to manifest our desires.

One layer within the law of attraction is visualization. Visualization is a powerful technique that involves creating mental images of our desires. By vividly imagining ourselves already in possession of what we desire, we create a strong energetic connection with our desires. Affirmations play a crucial role in amplifying the effectiveness of visualization by reinforcing positive beliefs and intentions.

Another layer within the law of attraction is emotional alignment. Our emotions are powerful indicators of our vibrational frequency. By aligning our emotions with the feelings of already having our desires, we elevate our energetic state and attract what we seek. Affirmations can help us cultivate positive emotions and maintain an aligned vibrational frequency.

The final layer within the law of attraction is action. While affirmations are a potent tool for manifestation, they are not a substitute for action. Taking inspired action towards our desires is essential for bringing them into physical reality. Affirmations can motivate and inspire us to take the necessary steps towards our goals.

To accelerate the manifestation process, there are techniques and methods that can be employed. These techniques involve contracting time and speeding up the realization of our desires. Affirmations play a significant role in this process. By repeatedly affirming our desires and maintaining a strong belief in their manifestation, we can collapse the timeline and witness rapid results.

Success stories and examples of individuals who have successfully manifested their desires quickly serve as inspiration and validation of the power of affirmations. These stories showcase the universe's response to thoughts and intentions. By directing our thoughts and intentions towards our desires through affirmations, we align ourselves with the energetic frequency required to attract what we seek.

Affirmations act as declarations of present manifestation. By affirming what is already present in our lives, we align our energy and beliefs with the manifestation of our desires. This alignment enhances the power of affirmations and reinforces our connection with the universe's response.

To effectively use affirmations as declarations of present manifestation, it is important to infuse them with unwavering belief and conviction. By wholeheartedly embracing the power of affirmations, we unlock the ultimate potential within ourselves and align ourselves with the limitless possibilities of the universe.

In conclusion, incorporating affirmations into our daily lives requires consistency, persistence, and a deep belief in their power. By becoming clear about what we want, writing clear and positive affirmations, seamlessly incorporating them into our daily routine, shifting our mindset and maintaining a positive focus, understanding the laws of attraction, mastering the different layers and categories within the law of attraction, accelerating the manifestation process, witnessing the universe's response, and using affirmations as declarations of present manifestation, we can harness the ultimate power of manifestation.

I encourage you, the reader, to start implementing these strategies in your daily routine. Embrace the potential within you and let affirmations become a guiding force in your journey towards manifestation. The power is in your hands, and with the right mindset, belief, and practice, you can tap into the unlimited power of affirmations to manifest your desires and create the life you truly desire.

Morning Affirmations: Setting the Tone for a Manifestation-Filled Day

When I wake up in the morning and the golden rays of the sun gently kiss my face, I know it's a moment filled with potential and opportunity. It's like the universe is whispering, "What will you manifest today?" And with a mix of excitement and anticipation, I begin my morning ritual of setting affirmations that will shape the trajectory of my day.

There's something magical about affirmations - those positive, empowering statements we tell ourselves in order to manifest our desires. They're not just words; they're a powerful tool for self-transformation and the fuel that propels our dreams into reality.

As I find a cozy corner in my room and close my eyes, I take a moment to ground myself in the present. With each breath, I let go of yesterday's worries and shift my focus to the infinite possibilities of today. And in this stillness, I begin to craft my morning affirmations.

I carefully choose words that resonate deeply with my aspirations and desires. They're not just a string of clichés; they're heartfelt declarations that align with the essence of who I truly am. Whether it's financial abundance, love, health, or career success, I trust my intuition to guide me towards the affirmations that will bring me closer to my dreams.

With a sense of conviction, I speak my affirmations aloud, infusing each word with intention and belief. I can feel the vibrational energy of my desires reverberating through my body, as if every cell is waking up and aligning with the truth of my affirmations. It's like I'm planting the seeds of my dreams, trusting that they will grow and blossom into my reality.

To amplify the power of my affirmations, I engage my senses. I visualize myself already in possession of my desires, feeling the joy, abundance, and success that they bring. I hear the laughter, see the smiling faces, and immerse myself in the emotions of my manifestations. By creating a vivid mental picture and engaging my senses, I'm imprinting these images and emotions into my subconscious mind, making the manifestation process even more potent.

I repeat my affirmations several times until I feel a sense of calm assurance washing over me. It's like a blanket of certainty that wraps around my heart and guides my actions throughout the day. I carry this newfound energy with me as I step out into the world, confident that the intentions I have set and the affirmations I have spoken will guide my path.

And as I go about my day, I am a living testament to the power of manifestation. I see synchronicities unfold before my eyes, opportunities knocking at my door, and miracles manifesting in the most unexpected ways. It's as if the universe is conspiring in my favor, aligning circumstances and people to support my journey towards my dreams.

With every morning affirmation, I am reminded of the divine power within me to co-create my reality. I am a conscious participant in the dance between my thoughts and the universe, knowing that I have the ability to shape my destiny. It's a humbling and empowering realization that propels me forward, one step closer to the life I envision.

So, today, and every day, I will continue to start my mornings with positive affirmations. I will honor the power of my thoughts and beliefs, knowing that they are the building blocks of my reality. With gratitude and trust, I surrender to the magic of the universe, eagerly awaiting the manifestation of my dreams.

For I am a divine being, a vessel for infinite possibilities. And as I infuse my days with the power of morning affirmations, I am a channel for miracles, abundance, and joy to flow effortlessly into my life.

Afternoon Affirmations: Maintaining Momentum and Focus

Hey there! Let's talk about the power of affirmations in the afternoon. Picture this: the sun is shining, and you're feeling good about the progress you've made on your manifestation journey so far. But how do you stay focused and maintain that positive mindset throughout the day? That's where afternoon affirmations come in.

Afternoon affirmations are like little boosts of motivation and alignment during those mid-day hours. They remind you of your desired reality and reinforce your belief in the manifestation process. By consciously repeating positive statements, you keep your mind focused on the positive, even when faced with distractions or challenges. They keep you motivated, energized, and on track with your manifestations.

Now, let's dive into some techniques to create impactful afternoon affirmations. The key here is to make sure your affirmations resonate deeply with your intentions and desires. Be specific and present with your statements. Instead of saying "I will be successful," say "I am successful in all areas of my life." This helps you align your affirmations with the present moment and creates a stronger connection to your desires.

Another tip is to use positive language. Frame your affirmations with positive words and avoid any negativity or limiting beliefs. Instead of saying "I am not anxious," say "I am calm and composed in every situation." The language you choose shapes your thoughts and beliefs, so it's important to keep it positive.

Emphasizing feelings is another powerful technique. Infuse your affirmations with the emotions and sensations you'll experience once your desires come true. By adding emotion, you intensify the magnetic force that attracts your desires to you. For example, say "I am filled with joy and gratitude as abundance flows effortlessly into my life." Feel the emotions, see the vivid details, and embrace the experience as if it's already happening.

Repetition and visualization are also key. Repeat your affirmations several times throughout the day to let them sink deep into your subconscious mind. And as you repeat them, visualize yourself already living the reality described in your affirmations. See it, feel it, embrace it. This combination of repetition and visualization strengthens the power of your affirmations.

Don't forget to tailor your affirmations to specific areas of your life that need attention. Whether it's love, career, health, or any other area, creating specific affirmations for each aspect gives your manifestation journey a more holistic approach.

By implementing these techniques, your afternoon affirmations become potent declarations that keep you focused, motivated, and connected to the energy of your desires. They remind you of the limitless potential within you and strengthen your belief in the manifestation process.

As you continue to practice afternoon affirmations, pay attention to the subtle shifts happening within you. Notice how your mindset becomes more resilient, your focus sharper, and your manifestations closer to reality. Embrace the power of positive self-talk and let it guide your thoughts and actions throughout the day. With each afternoon affirmation, you deepen your connection with the universe and direct your intentions towards the manifestation of your dreams.

In the next chapter, we'll explore the fascinating world of creative expression and how incorporating art and creativity into your manifestation practices can amplify your intentions and bring your desires to life. So, stay tuned for Chapter 9: Creative Expression: Using Art and Creativity for Manifestation.

I can't wait to share that with you!

Every night, as I prepare to drift off to sleep, I embark on a magical journey of reprogramming my subconscious mind through the practice of evening affirmations. It's an extraordinary experience that allows me to tap into the immense power of my thoughts and set the stage for manifesting my deepest desires as I slumber.

You might be wondering, why are evening affirmations so important? Well, let me tell you, my friend. The subconscious mind is like a secret vault, holding the key to unlocking our full potential. It tirelessly processes and makes sense of all the information it receives, operating on beliefs and patterns that have been deeply ingrained within us, often without our conscious awareness.

But here's the thing: those beliefs and patterns aren't always serving us well. They can often be limiting, holding us back from reaching our true potential. And that's where evening affirmations come in. They act as a way to override those negative thoughts and beliefs, rewiring our thinking patterns and creating new pathways that support our manifestations.

Crafting powerful evening affirmations is an intentional practice. Throughout the day, I pay close attention to my thoughts, especially the ones that are negative or limiting. I acknowledge them, but I don't let them define me. Instead, I challenge their validity and remind myself that they are remnants of old programming that no longer serves me.

With this newfound awareness, I create affirmations that directly counteract those negative beliefs. For example, if I find myself doubting my ability to attract financial abundance, I create an affirmation like this: "I am a magnet for wealth and prosperity. Money flows freely and abundantly into my life with ease." Every night before bed, I repeat this affirmation with conviction, gently implanting these positive thoughts into my subconscious mind.

Now, here's the secret to supercharging the effectiveness of evening affirmations: engaging all your senses. Before settling into bed, I transform my bedroom into a sanctuary of calm and tranquility. I dim the lights, ignite a scented candle or diffuse essential oils that promote relaxation, and play soothing instrumental music. These sensory cues heighten the impact of my affirmations, creating an atmosphere that amplifies their manifestation potential.

Once I'm snuggled under the covers, I take a moment to center myself. I take deep, grounding breaths, bringing my focus to the present moment. Then, I begin reciting my evening affirmations, speaking them with utmost conviction and pouring my emotions into each word. I visualize my desires as if they have already been manifested, feeling the profound joy and gratitude as if they're already a reality. This visualization technique further imprints the affirmations into my subconscious mind, intensifying their power to manifest.

As sleep envelops me, I surrender any attachment to the outcome. I release my intentions into the universe, knowing that the divine forces are at work, aligning everything in my favor. It's a peaceful surrender, a trusting dance with the cosmos, confident that my evening affirmations have planted the seeds of my desires deep within my subconscious mind.

And let me tell you, my friend, the results are awe-inspiring. I've witnessed the incredible power of evening affirmations in my own life as my manifestations effortlessly unfold before me. The subconscious mind doesn't just influence our beliefs and perceptions, but it also shapes our actions and attracts opportunities. By intentionally rewiring my subconscious mind through evening affirmations, I'm harnessing the full potential of my thoughts, emotions, and intentions to manifest my desires while I sleep.

In conclusion, the practice of evening affirmations is a profound tool for reprogramming the subconscious mind and manifesting our wildest dreams. By crafting powerful affirmations, engaging all our senses, and visualizing our desires, we tap into the limitless potential of our subconscious mind. Through this intentional practice, we're able to rewrite our thought patterns, align ourselves with the energy of manifestation, and create a profound transformation in our lives. So tonight, as you lay your head on the pillow, why not join me on this enchanting journey of evening affirmations, and witness the magic as your dreams manifest before your very eyes?

Chapter 10: The Power of Intuition

Developing Your Intuition

Intuition is a powerful tool that we all possess, yet many of us fail to tap into its potential. In this subchapter, we will explore the concept of intuition and its significance in decision-making. I will share techniques that can help you strengthen and trust your intuition, and highlight the benefits of developing this innate ability.

When we talk about intuition, we are referring to that gut feeling or instinct that guides us in making choices. It is that voice within us that seems to know the right path to take, even when we can't explain why. Developing our intuition is crucial because it allows us to access insights beyond our rational thinking. It taps into a deeper level of knowing, helping us make decisions that align with our true selves.

The focus of this subchapter is to provide you with practical techniques to strengthen and trust your intuition. We will dive into exercises that can enhance your intuitive abilities, such as mindfulness practices. By cultivating present moment awareness, you can quiet the noise of the mind and create space for intuitive insights to emerge.

Self-reflection and self-awareness are also key components in developing intuition. By taking the time to understand ourselves better, we can recognize the patterns and triggers that influence our decision-making. Journaling and meditation can be powerful tools in this process, helping us gain clarity and tap into our intuitive wisdom.

Trusting our intuition is another vital aspect of developing this ability. Doubts and skepticism often creep in, making us question the validity of our intuitive insights. However, when we learn to trust our intuition, we open ourselves up to a world of possibilities. We will explore strategies to build confidence in our intuitive abilities and provide examples of situations where trusting intuition has led to positive outcomes.

Of course, developing intuition is not without its challenges. Misconceptions and skepticism surround this innate ability, causing many to dismiss its power. Fear and self-doubt can also hinder our intuitive insights. In this subchapter, we will address these challenges head-on and provide suggestions for overcoming them. Embracing intuition as a valuable tool requires us to push past our comfort zones and trust in the wisdom that lies within us.

In conclusion, developing your intuition is a journey that can lead to incredible growth and transformation. By strengthening and trusting your intuition, you gain access to insights and guidance that can profoundly impact your life. In the following sections, we will delve deeper into the benefits of developing intuition, techniques for honing this skill, and the importance of trusting your intuitive instincts. Get ready to unlock the ultimate power of manifestation through the wisdom of your intuition.

Intuitive Decision Making

When it comes to making decisions, many of us rely heavily on logic, reasoning, and external factors. We analyze the pros and cons, weigh the options, and try to make the most informed choice possible. But what if I told you that there is another powerful tool at your disposal? Intuition, the inner voice that guides us towards what feels right, can be a game-changer when it comes to making aligned and empowered decisions.

Intuition has the remarkable ability to lead us towards choices that are in alignment with our true desires and goals. It taps into our subconscious mind, which is often more attuned to what we truly want than our conscious mind. By listening to our intuition, we can make decisions that resonate deeply with our authentic selves, leading to a sense of fulfillment and success.

The importance of intuitive decision making cannot be overstated. In a world filled with external noise and distractions, it is crucial to tap into our intuition to find clarity and make choices that truly serve us. Intuition has the power to cut through the noise and guide us towards what is truly important. Whether it is choosing a career path, deciding on a relationship, or making a major life change, intuition can be the guiding force that leads us towards the path of success and fulfillment.

The Importance of Tapping into Intuition:

Accessing and harnessing our intuition is not just a nice-to-have, it is essential for our personal growth and success. Intuition has a way of leading us towards more successful and fulfilling outcomes, often beyond what our logical mind can comprehend. When we tap into our intuition, we open ourselves up to possibilities and opportunities that we may have otherwise overlooked.

So how do we tap into our intuition? There are practical tips and techniques that can help us hone our intuitive abilities and use them to make better decisions. One such technique is meditation, which allows us to quiet the mind and listen to the whispers of our intuition. Another technique is journaling, where we can freely express our thoughts and feelings without judgment, allowing our intuition to come to the surface.

Trusting Your Gut:

Trusting our instincts and gut feelings is a crucial aspect of intuitive decision making. Our intuition often knows what is best for us, even when logic and reasoning may suggest otherwise. It is that inner knowing that nudges us in the right direction, guiding us towards choices that align with our true selves.

To illustrate the power of trusting our intuition, let me share a personal anecdote. A few years ago, I was faced with a career decision that seemed logical on paper. It offered stability, financial security, and all the checkboxes of a successful career. However, my intuition was telling me otherwise. Despite the logical arguments, something deep within me knew that this was not the path for me. I trusted my gut and made a different choice, and it turned out to be one of the best decisions I ever made. It led me towards a career that was aligned with my passions and brought me a sense of fulfillment that I had never experienced before.

Intuition as a Tool for Manifestation:

The connection between intuition and manifestation is undeniable. When we listen to our intuition and follow its guidance, we enhance the effectiveness and ease of our manifestation efforts. Intuition acts as a compass, pointing us towards the actions and decisions that will bring us closer to our desires.

There are countless examples and evidence supporting the relationship between intuition and successful manifestation. Think about those moments when you had a strong feeling that something would happen, and it did. Or those times when you followed a hunch and it led to a synchronistic event that aligned perfectly with your desires. These are all instances where intuition played a vital role in the manifestation process.

Developing Intuition for Manifestation:

To harness the power of intuition for manifestation, it is essential to develop and strengthen our intuitive abilities. Fortunately, there are practical exercises and techniques that can help us tap into our intuition specifically for the purpose of manifestation.

One technique is visualization. By vividly imagining our desires and the emotions associated with them, we create a clear mental image that our intuition can latch onto. Another technique is connecting with nature, which allows us to tap into the wisdom of the natural world and access our intuition. These are just a few examples of the many ways we can develop our intuition to enhance our manifestation abilities.

Real-life Examples of Intuitive Decision Making:

To truly grasp the transformative power of intuitive decision making, it is helpful to look at real-life examples of individuals who have successfully used their intuition to make empowered decisions and manifest their desires. These examples serve as both inspiration and guidance for readers to apply these principles in their own lives.

One such example is the story of Sarah, a woman who had been struggling with finding her purpose and creating a fulfilling career. Despite the pressure from society to pursue a traditional path, Sarah trusted her intuition and decided to start her own business in a field she was deeply passionate about. Against all odds, her business flourished, and she found a sense of fulfillment that she had never experienced before. Sarah's story is a testament to the power of intuitive decision making and the transformative impact it can have on our lives.

The Relationship Between Intuition and Alignment:

Intuition and alignment go hand in hand. Following our intuition ensures that our decisions are in alignment with our authentic selves and desires, leading to greater manifestation success. When we listen to our intuition, we tap into our true desires and make choices that resonate deeply with who we are.

Research has shown that individuals who trust their intuition and make decisions in alignment with their true selves are more likely to achieve their goals and manifest their desires. This connection between intuition and alignment is a powerful reminder of the importance of tapping into our intuition and using it as a guiding force in our manifestation journey.

Intuition as a Source of Wisdom:

Our intuition is not just a random gut feeling, it is a valuable source of insight and knowledge in the manifestation process. When we trust our intuition, we access a wellspring of wisdom that can provide unique perspectives and solutions to challenges.

Think about a time when you were faced with a difficult decision and your intuition guided you towards a solution that you had never considered before. That is the power of intuition as a source of wisdom. By trusting our intuition, we tap into a well of creativity and innovation that can propel us towards our manifestation goals.

Integrating Intuition with Manifestation Techniques:

Intuition and manifestation techniques are not mutually exclusive, they can work in synergy to enhance our manifestation results. Techniques such as visualization, affirmations, and gratitude practices can be integrated with our intuition to create a powerful manifestation practice.

For example, when practicing visualization, we can tap into our intuition to uncover any underlying limiting beliefs or resistance that may be hindering our manifestation efforts. By combining intuition with these techniques, we gain a deeper understanding of ourselves and can make the necessary shifts to align with our desires.

Unleashing the Power of Intuition in Manifestation:

The power of intuition in the manifestation process is immense. It is up to us to harness and trust our intuition to unlock our full manifestation potential. By listening to our intuition, we tap into a wellspring of guidance and wisdom that can lead us towards the creation of the desired life.

Intuitive decision making is not just about making choices, it is about creating a life that is in alignment with our true desires and goals. It is about trusting ourselves and following the whispers of our intuition, even when the world around us may suggest otherwise. When we embrace the power of intuition, we open ourselves up to a world of possibilities and embark on a journey of self-discovery and manifestation.

Intuition and Synchronicities

Intuition and synchronicities are two powerful forces that guide us through life. They are like hidden whispers from the Universe, nudging us towards the right path and helping us navigate the complex web of existence. In this chapter, we will explore the profound significance of recognizing and interpreting synchronicities as a means of manifesting our desires and transforming our lives.

Synchronicities, in essence, are meaningful coincidences that defy the laws of probability. They are the universe's way of communicating with us, offering signs and symbols that hold deeper messages. These occurrences often leave us in awe, as if we have stumbled upon something magical or mystical. But in reality, synchronicities are not mere chance happenings; they are the product of an intricate and interconnected web of energy that permeates the universe.

To better understand synchronicities, let's consider a few examples. Imagine you've been contemplating a major career change, unsure of whether to take the leap or play it safe. Suddenly, you come across an old friend who just so happens to work in your dream industry. This encounter feels like more than just a coincidence; it feels like the Universe is guiding you towards your true calling.

Or perhaps you've been struggling with a difficult decision and feeling overwhelmed. One day, while browsing through a bookstore, a particular book catches your eye. You pick it up, and as you read the back cover, you realize that its contents directly address the challenges you've been facing. This synchronicity acts as a gentle reminder from the Universe, affirming that you are on the right path and that the answers you seek are within reach.

Intuition plays a significant role in recognizing and interpreting synchronicities. It is the subtle inner voice that guides us, providing insight and wisdom beyond our logical reasoning. When we learn to trust our intuition, we open ourselves to a world of possibilities and synchronistic experiences. Our intuition acts as a bridge between the conscious and unconscious mind, allowing us to tap into a deeper level of awareness.

Synchronicities, in turn, serve as a confirmation of our intuitive knowing. They validate our instincts and reassure us that we are aligned with our true purpose. By paying attention to these synchronistic occurrences, we can gain valuable insights into our lives and make informed decisions that lead to our desired outcomes.

While some may dismiss synchronicities as mere coincidences, there is a growing body of evidence and research supporting the idea that they are indeed guidance from the Universe. Scientific studies have shown that synchronicities are not random occurrences, but rather meaningful patterns that reflect the interconnectedness of all things. Quantum physics, for example, suggests that there is a hidden order and intelligence underlying the fabric of reality, and synchronicities are manifestations of this invisible force.

However, it is important to address the skepticism that skeptics may have towards the concept of synchronicities as guidance. Some may argue that these occurrences are nothing more than our brains seeking patterns and connections where none exist. While it is true that our minds are wired to find meaning in chaos, it is the profound significance and personal relevance of synchronicities that sets them apart from ordinary coincidences.

Furthermore, it is crucial to acknowledge the limitations and criticisms of the concept of synchronicities as guidance. Not all synchronicities are positive or lead to desirable outcomes. Sometimes, they serve as cautionary signs or wake-up calls, urging us to reevaluate our choices or beliefs. Additionally, synchronicities are subjective experiences that can vary greatly from person to person, making it difficult to establish a universal framework for their interpretation.

Ultimately, synchronicities offer us a unique lens through which we can perceive the world and navigate our lives. They are not magical solutions or quick fixes, but rather invitations to deepen our understanding of ourselves and the world around us. By embracing synchronicities as guidance from the Universe, we tap into the ultimate power of manifestation and unlock infinite possibilities for growth and transformation.

Chapter 11: The Transformative Power of Gratitude

Cultivating a Gratitude Practice

Cultivating a gratitude practice is an essential aspect of manifestation. It is the process of intentionally focusing on the things we are grateful for and appreciating the abundance in our lives. By doing so, we can tap into the power of gratitude and manifest our desires more easily and quickly.

Research has shown that practicing gratitude has numerous benefits. One of the key benefits is achieving peace of mind. When we cultivate a gratitude practice, we train our minds to focus on the positive aspects of our lives, which in turn helps us find inner peace and contentment. By acknowledging and appreciating what we already have, we shift our focus away from what is lacking and create a sense of abundance.

Another benefit of practicing gratitude is increased control over our thoughts. When we regularly express gratitude, we become more aware of our thought patterns and can choose to redirect them towards positive and empowering thoughts. This can be especially helpful when it comes to manifestation because our thoughts play a crucial role in creating our reality. By consciously choosing thoughts of gratitude, we align ourselves with the frequency of abundance and attract more of what we desire.

The connection between gratitude and manifestation can be illustrated through various examples and stories. For instance, consider the story of Sarah, who wanted to manifest a promotion at work. Instead of focusing on the lack of recognition, she started a gratitude practice, expressing gratitude for her current job, her skills, and the opportunities she had. As she continued to cultivate gratitude, she noticed a shift in her mindset and energy. She became more confident, took inspired actions, and ultimately manifested the promotion she desired.

Finding a mentor or taking a course can greatly enhance our manifestation journey. A good mentor or course can provide guidance, support, and valuable insights into the manifestation process. By following their instructions and applying the knowledge gained, we can accelerate our manifestation results. It is important to find a mentor or course that resonates with us and aligns with our values and goals.

However, simply learning from a mentor or taking a course is not enough. It is crucial to take action and apply what we have learned. Knowledge without action is merely intellectual entertainment. To manifest our desires, we must take inspired actions and implement the strategies and techniques shared by our mentor or course. This requires dedication, discipline, and perseverance.

Gratitude and joy are powerful indicators of our capacity to receive what we desire. When we feel grateful and joyful, we align our energy with the frequency of abundance. We become open and receptive to the manifestations that are on their way to us. Therefore, it is essential to cultivate gratitude and joy as part of our manifestation practice.

Imagination and visualization are vital components of the manifestation process. By using our imagination, we can create a mental blueprint of our desires. Visualization allows us to see, feel, and experience our desired outcomes as if they have already manifested. This helps us align our thoughts and energy with our desires, making manifestation more effective.

Our thoughts play a significant role in the manifestation process. What we focus on expands, and our thoughts shape our reality. For example, if we constantly focus on lack and scarcity, we will attract more of the same. On the other hand, if we focus on abundance and gratitude, we will attract more abundance into our lives. Therefore, it is important to become mindful of our thoughts and consciously choose thoughts that align with our desires.

To fully immerse ourselves in the manifestation journey, it is crucial to study and learn continuously. By immersing ourselves in the study of manifestation, we deepen our understanding and gain new perspectives. Diligently applying the principles, we learn allows us to integrate them into our daily lives and experience transformative results.

Affirmations are powerful tools for attracting and transforming what we desire. They are positive statements that help reprogram our subconscious mind and align our thoughts with our desires. Effective affirmations are specific, positive, and in the present tense. By incorporating affirmations into our gratitude practice, we reinforce our intentions and attract what we want.

Incorporating gratitude practices into our daily routine is key to maximizing the benefits of manifestation. Consistency and regularity are essential in creating lasting change. Simple practices such as keeping a gratitude journal, expressing gratitude before meals, or practicing gratitude meditation can significantly enhance our manifestation journey. By making gratitude a daily habit, we create a positive mindset and attract more of what we desire into our lives.

In conclusion, cultivating a gratitude practice is crucial for manifestation. It allows us to achieve peace of mind, gain control over our thoughts, and manifest our desires more easily. Finding a mentor or taking a course can provide valuable guidance, but it is essential to take action and apply what we have learned. Gratitude and joy are indicators of our capacity to receive, and imagination and visualization help us align our energy with our desires. Our thoughts shape our reality, and continuous learning and growth are vital in the manifestation journey. Affirmations and incorporating gratitude into our daily routine further amplify our manifestation benefits. So, let us embrace the power of gratitude and unlock the ultimate power of manifestation.

Gratitude as a Manifestation Tool

Gratitude is a powerful tool that can greatly enhance our ability to manifest our desires. It is a concept that has been utilized for centuries by various cultures and spiritual practices, and its effectiveness has been supported by numerous research studies. In this chapter, I will delve into the benefits of gratitude and explain how practicing it can lead to a more fulfilled and abundant life.

When we express gratitude, we are essentially acknowledging and appreciating the things we have in our lives. This simple act of recognition has a profound impact on our manifestation efforts. It shifts our focus from what we lack to what we already possess, creating a mindset of abundance and attracting more positive experiences.

One of the key benefits of gratitude is the sense of peace and control it brings to our minds. By acknowledging the blessings we have, we cultivate a sense of contentment and satisfaction. This inner peace not only improves our overall well-being but also allows us to approach our desires from a place of abundance rather than desperation.

Gratitude also has the power to make us feel happy and increase our capacity to receive what we want. When we express gratitude, we are essentially sending a signal to the universe that we are ready and open to receiving more blessings. This positive energy resonates with the vibrations of our desires, aligning our energy with what we wish to manifest and making the process easier and quicker.

In addition to these emotional and energetic benefits, gratitude also has practical advantages. By practicing gratitude, we become more aware of the opportunities and resources available to us. We develop a keen eye for the abundance that surrounds us, and this newfound perspective allows us to make the most of what we have and attract more of what we desire.

Practicing gratitude is not limited to focusing on what we already have; it also involves expressing gratitude for the things we would like to have as if they are already ours. By adopting this mindset, we shift our focus from lack to possibility. We begin to embody the feelings and emotions associated with our desires, attracting them into our reality.

Even in challenging situations, there are always reasons to be grateful and joyful. It is during these times that the power of gratitude truly shines. By finding something positive to be grateful for, we shift our perspective and open ourselves up to new opportunities and solutions. We transform challenging situations into stepping stones for growth and manifestation.

In conclusion, gratitude is a vital tool for manifestation. It not only enhances our ability to attract what we desire but also brings a sense of peace, control, and abundance to our lives. By practicing gratitude, we align our energy with our desires, sending a positive signal to the universe and attracting more of what we wish to manifest. So, let us embrace the power of gratitude and watch as our desires manifest with ease and joy.

During challenging times, maintaining a positive mindset can often feel like an uphill battle. It's easy to become overwhelmed by the difficulties we face and to let negativity seep into our thoughts and emotions. However, it is during these trying times that the concept of gratitude becomes even more essential.

Gratitude, at its core, is about acknowledging and appreciating the good in our lives. It is about finding joy in the small moments and being thankful for the blessings we have, no matter how big or small. But why is gratitude so important, especially when times get tough?

When faced with challenges, it can be incredibly difficult to practice gratitude. The weight of our problems can feel all-consuming, making it hard to focus on anything positive. However, it is precisely in these moments that gratitude can become a powerful tool for resilience and manifestation.

By cultivating a gratitude practice, we shift our focus from what is going wrong to what is going right. We train ourselves to seek out the silver linings in tough situations and to find joy even in the midst of adversity. This shift in perspective not only helps us maintain a positive mindset, but it also provides us with the motivation and sense of hope necessary to persevere through difficult times.

But how do we maintain a gratitude practice when everything seems to be falling apart? There are several strategies and techniques that can help us stay grounded in gratitude, even when life feels like a never-ending storm.

One such strategy is keeping a gratitude journal. By writing down three things we are grateful for each day, we create a tangible reminder of the good in our lives. This simple practice forces us to actively seek out moments of gratitude, no matter how small they may seem. It also serves as a powerful tool for reflection, allowing us to revisit our entries during challenging times and reminding us of the abundance we have experienced in the past.

Another technique is practicing mindfulness. By staying present in the moment and fully experiencing our emotions, we become more attuned to the blessings that surround us. Mindfulness allows us to appreciate the beauty of everyday life, even when it feels like chaos is reigning supreme. It is through this heightened awareness that we can truly embrace gratitude and all its transformative power.

The benefits of practicing gratitude during challenging times are numerous. Not only does it increase our resilience, allowing us to bounce back from adversity with grace and strength, but it also enables us to find meaning and purpose in even the most difficult circumstances. By focusing on the positive, we open ourselves up to new opportunities and invite abundance into our lives.

This concept of abundance leads us to the idea of manifestation. Manifestation is the belief that we have the power to attract positive outcomes and experiences into our lives through our thoughts and actions. And gratitude, my friends, is one of the most powerful tools we have for manifesting these positive outcomes, even in the face of adversity.

When we practice gratitude, we align ourselves with the energy of abundance. We send a signal to the universe that we are open to receiving more of what we are grateful for. This, in turn, attracts more positivity into our lives, amplifying our ability to manifest the things we desire.

But it doesn't stop there. The true power of gratitude lies in its ability to transform our lives. When we fully embrace gratitude and make it a consistent practice, something magical happens. We begin to realize just how much power we have over our own happiness and success.

Throughout history, countless individuals have used gratitude as a tool for resilience and manifestation. Their stories serve as powerful examples of the transformative power of gratitude. From entrepreneurs who have turned failure into success, to individuals who have overcome unimaginable adversity, their journeys are a testament to the profound impact of gratitude.

As with any practice, maintaining a gratitude practice during challenging times can come with its own set of challenges. It's easy to get caught up in the negativity and lose sight of the good. But by acknowledging these obstacles and finding strategies to overcome them, we can ensure that our gratitude practice remains steadfast.

Whether it's creating a daily routine, seeking support from loved ones, or finding alternative ways to express gratitude, there are always solutions available to us. By being proactive and finding ways to overcome these challenges, we can continue to reap the benefits of gratitude, even during the most trying times.

In conclusion, maintaining a gratitude practice during challenging times is not only possible, but it is also essential for personal growth, resilience, and manifestation. It allows us to shift our focus from negativity to positivity, enabling us to find joy even in the midst of adversity. By adopting a mindset of gratitude, we open ourselves up to a world of abundance and limitless possibilities. So, my friends, let us embrace gratitude and harness its ultimate power of manifestation.

Gratitude and Abundance

The Science of Gratitude

Gratitude, my friend, is like magic. It has this incredible ability to turn our lives around in the most extraordinary ways. And let me tell you, it all starts in our brains. I mean, who would've thought that a simple act of expressing gratitude can set off a whole rewiring process in our heads? But hey, science doesn't lie!

So, picture this: when we practice gratitude, our brains go into overdrive. Like, seriously, several areas of our brains light up like Fourth of July fireworks. One of these areas is called the prefrontal cortex, which basically rules the roost when it comes to decision-making, emotions, and long-term memories. By activating this part of our brain with gratitude, we're like connecting all the dots, you know? It's like the ultimate team-building exercise for our brain.

And it's not just about the brain activity; it's the chemicals too. Gratitude triggers the release of some super feel-good chemicals, like dopamine and serotonin. These little dudes are responsible for giving us those warm fuzzies of happiness, contentment, and overall well-being. The best part? The more we practice gratitude, the better our brain becomes at producing these chemicals. Talk about a positive feedback loop!

But that's not all. Gratitude is like a superpower that extends its reach beyond our emotions. It's been proven that grateful people actually have stronger immune systems, lower blood pressure, and healthier hearts. I mean, who knew that being grateful could keep us physically healthy too? It's like gratitude is on a mission to kick stress right in the butt and keep our bodies running like well-oiled machines.

But let's get back to our brains for a minute. You see, gratitude is not just about feeling warm and fuzzy; it's about rewiring our brains for abundance. It's about shifting our perspective from lack and scarcity to recognizing the abundance that already exists in our lives. And when we do that, our brain starts sending signals to our subconscious, activating this thing called the reticular activating system (RAS). Fancy name, huh? Well, this RAS is like a super filter that helps us focus on the good stuff – opportunities, resources, and those crazy synchronicities that align perfectly with our desires.

It's like gratitude becomes this secret decoder ring that helps us see the world in a whole new light. And the more we focus on what we're grateful for, the more our brains get rewired to attract more of the good stuff. It's like a never-ending cycle of abundance – the kind that makes you feel like you're riding a unicorn through a rainbow. Okay, maybe not that extreme, but you get what I'm saying.

Now, here's the kicker: to really tap into the true power of gratitude, we got to make it a daily practice. It's not a one-and-done kind of deal. We got to set aside a few minutes each day to reflect on what we're grateful for. Maybe it's the amazing people in our lives, the beauty of nature, or simply the fact that we're alive and kicking. And hey, write it down, speak it out loud, or just soak it in through meditation. It's all about cultivating that genuine sense of appreciation and letting it seep into every fiber of our being.

So, my friend, it's time to embrace gratitude like never before. It's time to let it wash over us and transform our lives into something truly magical. The power of manifestation is within each and every one of us, and gratitude is the key that unlocks it. So, let's hold onto that key with all our might and watch as our lives become a beautiful tapestry of blessings and opportunities.

Remember, my friend, gratitude is a choice – one that has the power to change our lives in ways we can only imagine. So, what are you waiting for? Let's dive into gratitude and create a world of endless abundance.

Cultivating a Gratitude Practice

Embracing the Power of Gratitude

Hey there! Let me tell you about this incredible tool that can totally upgrade your manifestation game – gratitude. It's mind-blowing how something as simple as being grateful can open up doors to abundance and happiness. So, buckle up and get ready for a gratitude journey like no other!

Exercise 1: Gratitude Journaling

Picture this: it's a cozy evening, and you're sitting with a dedicated journal just for gratitude. You pen down the things that made you smile that day, whether it was savoring a warm cup of tea or receiving a thoughtful text. As you write, you feel the goodness flow through you, brewing up a sense of joy and appreciation. With each entry, you're rewiring your brain to focus on the positives, attracting even more reasons to be grateful. It's like creating this magical loop of endless goodness!

Exercise 2: Gratitude Meditation

Now let's dive into the realm of meditation. Find a quiet spot, shut those peepers, and take a deep breath. As you become aware of the sensations in your body and the thoughts whizzing by, shift your focus to gratitude. Start with three things you're grateful for—a loving family, life-changing opportunities, or those precious life lessons. Allow those warm, fuzzy feelings to envelope you, spreading through your entire being. And guess what? You don't have to stop at three! Keep adding to your gratitude list, and watch as those peaceful vibes fill every nook and cranny of your soul.

Exercise 3: Acts of Gratitude

Gratitude isn't just about writing or meditation; it's about putting it into action! So, how about brightening someone's day with a random act of kindness? It could be a heartfelt note, a small surprise, or simply spending time with someone you treasure. By showering others with gratitude, you not only bring a smile to their face but also create this powerful ripple effect. The universe notices, and more reasons for gratitude start finding their way into your life. It's a win-win situation!

Exercise 4: Gratitude Walk

Ah, nature—the ultimate source of peace and wonder. Take a leisurely stroll in a park or garden, and let Mother Earth work her magic. As you inhale the sweet scent of flowers and witness the vibrant colors around you, feel your heart fill with gratitude. Allow yourself to become one with nature, realizing the interconnectedness of all things. With each step you take, gratitude blooms within, reinforcing your connection to the universe and its infinite abundance.

Imagine a life where gratitude becomes your superpower, manifesting miracles left and right. By adopting a gratitude practice with journaling, meditation, acts of gratitude, and nature connection, your turbo-charging your manifestation journey. So, dive in, embrace this practice wholeheartedly, and get ready for a mind-blowing transformation. Trust me, the universe has some unbelievable surprises in store for you!

Manifesting Abundance Through Gratitude

Hey there! Have you ever stopped to think about the power of gratitude? I mean, really think about it. It's crazy how something so simple can completely transform your life.

Let me tell you a little story. I used to be someone who was always focused on what I didn't have. My mind would constantly be filled with thoughts of lack and scarcity. Can you relate? But then, one day, something clicked. I realized that by shifting my focus to what I did have and expressing appreciation for it, I could attract even more positivity into my life.

And that's where gratitude comes in. It's about taking a moment to truly acknowledge and appreciate the blessings and positive aspects of your life. It's about shifting your energy and vibration to align with abundance.

Think about it. What you focus on expands, right? So, by practicing gratitude, you're essentially sending out a signal to the universe that says, "Hey, I appreciate what I have, and I'm ready for more!" And guess what? The universe listens and starts sending more opportunities, resources, and abundance your way.

So, how can you incorporate gratitude into your daily life? Well, it's actually pretty simple. Start by setting aside a few moments each day to reflect on the things you're grateful for. It could be as quick as making a mental list or as intentional as writing them down in a gratitude journal. The important thing is to truly feel the gratitude in your heart.

And it doesn't stop there. You can infuse gratitude into your daily activities too. So, while you're preparing your meals, take a moment to appreciate the nourishment and sustenance that food provides. And when you're interacting with others, express your gratitude for their presence and the positive impact they have on your life.

You can even bring gratitude into your visualizations and affirmations. Imagine yourself in a state of deep gratitude, as if you've already manifested your desires. Feel the joy and appreciation as if it's already yours. And when affirming your desires, incorporate gratitude into your statements. For example, instead of saying, "I am abundant," say, "I am grateful for the abundance that flows into my life."

By incorporating gratitude into your manifestation practice, you're not only shifting your energy and perspective, but you're also deepening your connection to the abundant universe. And trust me, when you embrace a mindset of gratitude, you become more open and receptive to the abundance that's already flowing into your life.

So, my friend, start cultivating gratitude in your life today. Create a daily gratitude practice, infuse it into your daily activities, and incorporate it into your visualizations and affirmations. You'll be amazed at how gratitude can transform your life and help you experience the true power of manifestation.

Chapter 12: The Power of Words in Manifesting Love and Intimacy

The Art of Seductive Words

Effective communication is the cornerstone of any successful relationship. It is through our words that we express our desires, connect on a deeper level, and foster intimacy. However, there is a power beyond ordinary language, a power that lies in the seductive and romantic words we choose to use. These words have the ability to ignite desire and passion, creating a profound connection between two individuals.

In understanding the importance of seductive and romantic words, we must first recognize the impact they have on our psychological well-being. The mere utterance of these words can stir up excitement, anticipation, and arousal within us. It taps into our deepest desires, awakening a sense of longing that cannot be easily ignored. By understanding the psychological impact of seductive words, we can harness their power to create a more fulfilling and passionate relationship.

Cultural context also plays a significant role in the use and acceptance of seductive words. Different cultures have varying norms and expectations when it comes to expressing desire and passion. Exploring these cultural differences allows us to understand how societal norms shape our expression of seductive words. By recognizing and respecting these differences, we can navigate the intricacies of communication in a multicultural world.

Literature and poetry have long been used as mediums to express seductive and romantic words. The power of erotic literature and poetry lies in their ability to create a sensual and provocative experience for the reader. Through the use of literary devices and techniques such as metaphors, imagery, and figurative language, writers are able to transport their readers into a world of desire and passion. By examining these techniques, we can learn to infuse our own conversations with the art of seductive words.

It is not just in the realm of literature and poetry that seductive words find their place. They can be integrated into everyday conversations, enhancing intimacy and desire in our relationships. By understanding how to effectively incorporate seductive words into our communication, we can create a heightened sense of connection with our partners. Tips and strategies for using seductive words in everyday conversations will be explored, providing practical tools to enrich our relationships.

Language styles and techniques are diverse, offering us various ways to convey seductive and romantic messages. Through the use of metaphors, imagery, and figurative language, we can create a seductive atmosphere that captivates and entices our partners. By exploring these different language styles and techniques, we can expand our repertoire of seductive words, enhancing our ability to express desire and passion.

Gender dynamics also play a crucial role in the use and reception of seductive words. It is important to navigate these dynamics with sensitivity and respect, recognizing the power dynamics at play. Consent is of utmost importance when using seductive language, and it is crucial to consider the boundaries and comfort levels of both parties involved. By exploring the interplay of gender dynamics in the use of seductive words, we can cultivate a space of mutual desire and respect.

Timing and delivery are essential when it comes to the use of seductive words. The context, tone, and nonverbal cues can either enhance or detract from the seductive message. By understanding the art of timing and delivery, we can maximize the impact of our seductive words, creating an atmosphere of heightened intimacy and desire.

Beyond the superficial aspects of desire and passion, seductive words have the power to build emotional connection in a relationship. By expressing our desires in a vulnerable and honest manner, we foster trust and emotional intimacy with our partners. Understanding how seductive words can nurture emotional connection and intimacy allows us to create a deeper and more meaningful bond.

Finally, it is important to consider the ethics of using seductive words in relationships. Consent, boundaries, and communication are crucial aspects to navigate when engaging in seductive language. It is imperative to always prioritize the well-being and comfort of our partners, ensuring that our words enhance their experience rather than detract from it. By exploring the ethics of using seductive words, we can foster healthy and fulfilling relationships built on mutual respect and understanding.

In conclusion, the power of seductive and romantic words lies in their ability to ignite desire and passion in a relationship. By understanding the psychological impact, cultural context, and art of using seductive words, we can enhance intimacy and connection with our partners. Navigating gender dynamics, mastering timing and delivery, and building emotional connection through seductive words all contribute to creating a fulfilling and passionate relationship. However, it is crucial to always approach the use of seductive words with ethics and respect, ensuring that our words enhance the experience for both parties involved.

Communicating Love and Affection

In this subchapter, I want to delve into the importance of expressing love and affection through words in order to strengthen the bond with your partner. Let's analyze the pros and cons of this communication method and understand its relevance in building a strong and healthy relationship.

First, let's explore the benefits of expressing love and affection through words. One of the most significant advantages is that it enhances the emotional connection between partners. When you verbalize your love and affection, it allows both of you to connect on a deeper level, fostering a sense of intimacy and understanding. This, in turn, creates a stronger bond between you and your partner.

Additionally, expressing love and affection through words can boost your partner's self-esteem. When you openly express your love and appreciation for them, it reassures them of your feelings and reinforces their self-worth. This boost in self-esteem can have a profound impact on your relationship, leading to a more confident and fulfilling partnership.

Furthermore, verbal expressions of love and affection provide reassurance and security. Hearing these words from your partner reassures you of their commitment and loyalty, creating a sense of safety within the relationship. This can help to reduce doubts and insecurities, allowing both partners to feel more at ease and confident in their love for each other.

Another advantage of verbalizing love and affection is that it encourages open communication. When partners express their emotions through words, it creates a safe space for both individuals to express their needs and desires. This fosters a healthier and more transparent relationship, where both partners feel comfortable sharing their thoughts and emotions openly.

On the flip side, there are some potential drawbacks to consider. One of them is the risk of inauthentic expressions. Verbal expressions of love and affection can sometimes come across as superficial or insincere if they are not backed up by genuine emotions and actions. It's important to ensure that your words align with your true feelings in order to strengthen the bond between partners.

Miscommunication and misunderstandings are another potential downside. The way love and affection are communicated can vary from person to person, and words can be interpreted differently. This can lead to miscommunication and tension in the relationship, potentially straining the bond between partners.

Additionally, relying solely on verbal expressions of love and affection may neglect other important aspects of a relationship, such as physical touch, quality time, and acts of service. Neglecting these aspects can create an imbalance and potentially weaken the bond between partners.

Another limitation of verbal communication is the lack of non-verbal cues. Facial expressions, body language, and tone of voice are essential in conveying love and affection, and their absence in verbal communication can be limiting. It's important to remember that words alone may not fully capture the depth of your emotions.

Despite these potential drawbacks, there are still several positive aspects to consider. Expressing love and affection through words creates a positive and loving atmosphere in the relationship. It sets a tone of appreciation and gratitude, which can contribute to a happier and more fulfilling partnership.

Verbalizing love and affection also promote emotional vulnerability. It requires opening up and expressing deep emotions, fostering trust and allowing partners to feel safe in sharing their true selves. This vulnerability leads to a stronger emotional connection, further strengthening the bond between partners.

Furthermore, regularly expressing love and affection through words reinforces the commitment to each other. It serves as a reminder of the love and dedication shared, solidifying the bond and deepening the connection between partners.

Lastly, when one partner consistently expresses love and affection through words, it often encourages the other partner to reciprocate. This reciprocal expression of love creates a cycle of positivity and reinforces the bond between partners.

However, it's important to acknowledge that not everyone's love language aligns with verbal expressions. People have different ways of giving and receiving love, known as love languages. Verbal expressions of love and affection may not resonate as strongly with your partner if it's not their primary love language.

Moreover, overusing words to express love and affection can dilute their impact over time. When these words are constantly used, they may lose their sincerity and fail to create the desired emotional connection.

Additionally, language barriers can pose a challenge in multicultural relationships or relationships where partners have different native languages. Verbal communication of love and affection may face obstacles, limiting the effectiveness of this communication method and requiring alternative ways to express emotions.

By carefully analyzing the pros and cons of expressing love and affection through words, we can gain a deeper understanding of its significance in strengthening the bond with our partners. This analysis equips us with the knowledge to effectively communicate our feelings and build a stronger, more loving relationship.

Healing Words for Relationship Repair

In this subchapter, we delve into the power of healing words in relationship repair. It is my aim to explore how these words can mend wounds, resolve conflicts, and restore trust in a relationship. By understanding the background and context, we can grasp the significance of healing words in these transformative processes.

Comparison:

Healing words possess a unique ability to repair relationships. They have the power to transform the dynamics between individuals, fostering understanding, empathy, and connection. Research studies and evidence further support the effectiveness of healing words in repairing relationships, providing us with a solid foundation for exploration.

Using healing words to mend wounds in a relationship involves specific techniques and examples. By addressing past hurts and wounds with empathy, validation, and understanding, we can lay the groundwork for healing through words. These essential components enable the process of reconciliation and growth.

Conflicts within relationships can be defused and effectively communicated through the use of healing words. Active listening, nonviolent communication, and positive language are strategies that promote resolution and understanding. By implementing these techniques, conflicts can be resolved, and relationships can be strengthened.

Restoring trust in a damaged relationship requires the use of healing words. Honesty, accountability, and reassurance play crucial roles in rebuilding trust through words. By understanding how healing words can rebuild trust, we gain insight into the path towards a healthier relationship.

Contrast:

While healing words have significant power, it is important to acknowledge their limitations in repairing relationships. Solely relying on healing words may present challenges, as consistent actions and behaviors are necessary to complement the impact of words. This contrast reminds us that the journey towards relationship repair extends beyond words alone.

Addressing deeper underlying issues in addition to using healing words is crucial for comprehensive relationship repair. Therapy, self-reflection, and personal growth all play essential roles in the healing process. By delving into these deeper issues, individuals can truly understand and address the root causes of conflict.

Forgiveness, a vital component of relationship repair, requires more than just healing words. Genuine remorse and change are necessary for forgiveness to occur. Understanding forgiveness as a process reminds us that healing words must be backed by tangible actions and a genuine desire to change.

Sustaining relationship repair necessitates ongoing effort and commitment beyond the initial use of healing words. Continued communication, vulnerability, and emotional support are essential for maintaining a strong and healthy relationship. By recognizing the importance of these aspects, we can ensure that relationship repair goes beyond mere words.

The long-term benefits of consistently using healing words in relationship repair cannot be understated. By harnessing the power of healing words consistently, relationships can become healthier and more fulfilling. This understanding motivates us to continue utilizing healing words for long-term relationship success.

The power of healing words extends beyond relationship repair; they can also prevent future conflicts. By creating a foundation of open communication through healing words, conflicts can be minimized and even avoided altogether. Positive affirmations, encouragement, and appreciation all contribute to maintaining a strong and resilient relationship.

Cultivating a culture of healing words within a relationship requires mutual respect, emotional intelligence, and effective conflict resolution skills. By establishing and maintaining such a culture, relationships can flourish and withstand challenges.

Healing words not only facilitate relationship repair but also foster personal growth and self-awareness in individuals. By using healing words, individuals can undergo personal growth, leading to a deeper understanding of themselves and their relationships. This personal growth further contributes to relationship repair and overall relationship satisfaction.

In conclusion, the power of healing words for relationship repair cannot be overstated. By harnessing this power, we have the opportunity to mend wounds, resolve conflicts, and restore trust in our relationships. It is through the consistent use of healing words that we can cultivate a culture of understanding, empathy, and love.

Chapter 13: The Power of Action

Taking Aligned Action

In the journey of manifestation, one aspect that holds immense importance is taking aligned action. It is the crucial link that bridges the gap between our desires and their manifestation. When we align our actions with our desires, we unlock a powerful force that propels us towards the attainment of our goals.

Understanding the importance of aligned action is key to successful manifestation. It is not enough to simply visualize or affirm our desires; we must also take tangible steps in the direction of those desires. This is because taking action that aligns with our desires increases the likelihood of achieving the outcomes we seek.

Imagine a scenario where you desire financial abundance. You visualize and affirm wealth every day, but you do nothing to align your actions with that desire. In this case, the manifestation process becomes stagnant. However, when you take action that aligns with your desire for financial abundance, such as investing wisely or starting a business, you create momentum towards your goals. Aligned action accelerates the manifestation process, creating a powerful synergy between your intentions and your actions.

Understanding the connection between our actions and our desires is crucial. When we align our actions with our desires, we send a clear message to the universe about what we want to manifest. This focused and intentional approach helps us stay on track and eliminate distractions that could hinder our progress. By taking aligned action, we demonstrate our commitment to the manifestation process and signal our readiness to receive the desired outcomes.

Aligning actions with desires is not just a means to manifest goals effectively; it is a gateway to unlocking the ultimate power of manifestation. When we take action that aligns with our desires, we tap into a wellspring of manifestation potential. It is through aligned action that we transform our dreams into reality, bringing them from the realm of imagination into the physical world.

The impact of aligned action on desired outcomes cannot be underestimated. It sets the stage for success in manifesting goals. By aligning our actions with our desires, we create a harmonious flow of energy that attracts the opportunities and resources needed for manifestation. Aligned action serves as the catalyst for desired outcomes, propelling us towards the achievement of our goals.

To harness the ultimate power of manifestation, we must embrace the importance of aligning our actions with our desires. It is through this alignment that we unlock our true potential and manifest our deepest desires. By taking action that aligns with our desires, we create a powerful synergy that accelerates the manifestation process and brings us closer to our goals.

Understanding the significance of alignment is crucial. It is the foundation upon which intentional and impactful actions are built. When we are aware of the importance of taking action that aligns with our desires, we become more intentional in our choices and actions. This heightened awareness leads to a more focused and effective manifestation process, where every action we take moves us closer to our desired goals.

Aligned action plays a pivotal role in the manifestation process. It is the driving force that propels us towards our desired outcomes. By aligning our actions with our desires, we create a powerful momentum that carries us forward on our journey. It is through aligned action that we become active participants in the manifestation process, co-creating our reality with the universe.

To unlock the ultimate power of manifestation, we must fully embrace the concept of aligned action. It is the key that unlocks the door to our dreams. By aligning our actions with our desires, we create a potent synergy that accelerates the manifestation process and brings us closer to our goals. Through aligned action, we tap into the limitless potential within us and manifest a reality that surpasses our wildest dreams.

Overcoming Resistance to Action

Resistance and fear are two powerful barriers that often prevent us from taking action in our lives. They can hold us back from pursuing our dreams, achieving our goals, and living a fulfilled life. It is crucial for us to understand and overcome these barriers if we want to unlock the power of manifestation. In this literature review, I will provide strategies and insights into overcoming resistance and fear, allowing us to harness the ultimate power of manifestation.

Psychological factors play a significant role in creating resistance and fear. Fear of failure, self-doubt, and perfectionism are common psychological factors that hinder action. Fear of failure can paralyze us, making us doubt our abilities and preventing us from taking risks. Self-doubt can make us question our worthiness and capability, leading us to believe that we are not deserving of success. Perfectionism sets unrealistic standards for ourselves, making it impossible to take action unless everything is flawless.

To illustrate these psychological factors, let me share a case study of Sarah. Sarah had a dream of starting her own business but was crippled by fear of failure. Every time she thought about taking the first step, she was overwhelmed by self-doubt and worried that she would never be good enough. This fear and self-doubt held her back for years until she finally sought help to overcome them.

Understanding the impact of past experiences is crucial in overcoming resistance. Traumatic events, past failures, and negative feedback can create deep-rooted resistance within us. These experiences shape our beliefs about ourselves and our abilities. To move forward, we must address and overcome these past experiences. By doing so, we can release the hold they have on us and open ourselves up to new possibilities.

Cognitive strategies are powerful tools in overcoming resistance and fear. Positive thinking, reframing negative beliefs, and self-affirmation are all cognitive strategies that can shift our mindset and empower us to take action. By focusing on the positive aspects of our goals and reframing negative beliefs into positive ones, we can build confidence and belief in ourselves. Practical exercises such as visualization, affirmations, and goal-setting techniques can help us implement these cognitive strategies effectively.

Emotional strategies are equally important in overcoming resistance and fear. Managing emotions such as anxiety, fear, and overwhelm is crucial in taking action. Self-care, stress reduction techniques, and seeking support from others can help us regulate our emotions and create a supportive environment. By taking care of our emotional well-being, we can reduce the intensity of our resistance and fear, allowing us to take action with greater ease.

Behavioral strategies provide a roadmap for overcoming resistance and fear. Gradual exposure and taking small steps towards action can build momentum and confidence. Setting goals, implementing accountability systems, and managing our time effectively are all behavioral strategies that can propel us forward. Let's take the example of public speaking, a common fear for many. By gradually exposing ourselves to speaking in front of others and practicing regularly, we can overcome our fear and build confidence in this area.

Mindset plays a pivotal role in overcoming resistance and fear. Adopting a growth mindset, which embraces challenges and sees failures as opportunities for growth, fosters resilience and perseverance. By changing our mindset and beliefs about ourselves, we can overcome the barriers that resistance and fear create. Let me share the story of John, who transformed his mindset from one of self-doubt to one of self-belief. With this newfound mindset, John was able to overcome his resistance and fear, allowing him to achieve remarkable success.

External factors and support systems are crucial in overcoming resistance. Surrounding ourselves with a supportive environment, mentors, and peer accountability can provide the necessary motivation and guidance. By seeking and utilizing external support, we can tap into the collective wisdom and experiences of others who have overcome similar challenges.

Overcoming specific types of resistance requires targeted strategies and resources. Whether it is fear of public speaking or fear of rejection, there are tips, techniques, and resources available to help us overcome these specific situations. Practicing and building confidence in these areas is essential to overcoming the resistance they create.

In conclusion, this literature review has explored various strategies and insights into overcoming resistance and fear. By understanding the psychological factors, addressing past experiences, employing cognitive, emotional, and behavioral strategies, adopting the right mindset, utilizing external support, and targeting specific types of resistance, we can unlock the ultimate power of manifestation in our lives. It is now up to you, the reader, to take action and implement these strategies to overcome resistance and fear, and manifest the life you desire.

When it comes to manifesting our desires and creating the life we truly want, there is a powerful force that we often overlook - the flow of action. Embracing this flow means surrendering to the process and trusting in the guidance of the Universe. It requires us to let go of our need for control and certainty, and instead allow ourselves to be open to the opportunities and possibilities that come our way.

In a society that values action and productivity, the idea of surrendering may seem counterintuitive. We are conditioned to believe that success comes from our own efforts and that we have to take charge of every aspect of our lives. But the truth is, there is a greater wisdom at play. When we surrender to the flow of action, we tap into a higher power that knows what is best for us.

Understanding the Resistance to Surrender:

Many of us resist surrendering to the flow of action because we are afraid. We fear that by letting go, we will lose control over our lives and that things will not turn out the way we want them to. We also struggle with control issues, wanting to manipulate every situation to our advantage. Additionally, the desire for certainty often holds us back. We crave guarantees and assurances before we are willing to take a leap of faith.

Recognizing the Signs of Resistance:

Resistance can manifest in various ways - in our thoughts, emotions, and actions. We may find ourselves constantly questioning and doubting the process, or feeling anxious and stressed about the outcomes. Our actions may reflect our resistance through procrastination, self-sabotage, or clinging onto old patterns and behaviors. It is important to be aware of these signs, as they can indicate areas where we need to surrender and let go.

The Power of Letting Go:

Letting go and surrendering to the flow of action is incredibly powerful. It allows us to release the burden of control and open ourselves up to new possibilities. When we let go, we reduce stress and anxiety, as we no longer carry the weight of trying to orchestrate every detail. We create space for positive outcomes to unfold naturally, trusting that the Universe has our best interests at heart. Letting go is not a sign of weakness, but rather a recognition of the greater wisdom that exists beyond our limited understanding.

Cultivating Trust in the Universe:

To embrace the flow of action, we must cultivate trust in the Universe's guidance. This trust is not blind faith, but a deep knowing that there is a divine plan unfolding. One way to build trust is through meditation. By quieting our minds and connecting with our inner selves, we can tap into the universal wisdom that is always available to us. Affirmations and visualization exercises can also help us reinforce our trust and surrender to the process.

Learning from Past Experiences:

Reflecting on past situations where surrendering led to positive outcomes can be a powerful reminder of the transformative power of letting go. Whether it's a personal story or a case study, these examples serve as evidence that surrendering to the flow of action works. By studying these experiences, we can gain insights and lessons that can inform our own surrendering process.

Aligning with the Flow of Action:

Aligning our desires and goals with the Universe's guidance is crucial for manifestation. This requires self-awareness, intuition, and mindfulness. We must learn to listen to our inner voice and pay attention to the signs and synchronicities that the Universe presents to us. When we align our intentions with the flow of action, we become co-creators of our reality, working in harmony with the greater forces at play.

Overcoming Control Issues:

Releasing the need for control and embracing uncertainty is essential for manifestation. Trying to control every aspect of our lives limits our potential and prevents us from experiencing the full magic of surrendering. By surrendering, we create space for miracles to occur and for the Universe to work its magic. It requires a shift in mindset, letting go of the belief that we have to do everything ourselves.

Taking Inspired Action:

While surrendering is important, it doesn't mean we sit back and do nothing. Taking inspired action is about being open to opportunities and following the guidance that comes our way. It is about trusting our instincts and stepping out of our comfort zones when the time is right. When we take inspired action, we align ourselves with the flow of action and create momentum towards our desires.

Embracing Patience and Detachment:

Patience and detachment are crucial in the process of surrendering to the flow of action. It is easy to become impatient and attached to specific outcomes, but this only creates resistance. By cultivating patience, we allow the Universe to work in its own divine timing. Detachment allows us to surrender our attachment to the outcome, knowing that whatever unfolds is for our highest good. Practical tips and techniques, such as mindfulness practices and visualization, can help us nurture these qualities.

Nurturing a Positive Mindset:

A positive mindset is essential in embracing the flow of action and surrendering. By focusing on the positive aspects of our journey, we attract more positive experiences and outcomes. It is important to overcome negative thoughts or doubts that may arise, and instead, replace them with empowering beliefs and affirmations. Nurturing a positive mindset requires practice and self-awareness, but it is a powerful tool in manifesting our desires.

Conclusion and Encouragement:

In conclusion, embracing the flow of action and surrendering to the process is the ultimate power of manifestation. By surrendering, we tap into the wisdom of the Universe and allow it to guide us towards our desires. It requires trust, patience, and a willingness to let go of control. I encourage you to embrace this power and surrender to the flow of action, knowing that the Universe is always working in your favor. Trust in the process, and watch as miracles unfold in your life.

Chapter 14: The Abundance Mindset

Overcoming Scarcity Mentality

Hey there, ready to dive into the concept of scarcity mentality? I know, it sounds like a real downer, but bear with me because understanding this mindset can totally turn your manifestation game around. So, scarcity mentality is all about focusing on lack, limitation, and fear. It's like this constant belief that there's never enough to go around and we have to struggle our way through life just to get by. But here's the kicker - this mindset is seriously holding us back from manifesting abundance in our lives.

It's wild how ingrained this scarcity mentality is in our society, isn't it? I mean, we're bombarded with messages every day telling us that we need to work harder, buy more stuff, and compete with everyone else just to get our piece of the pie. And you know what? That mindset just breeds fear and insecurity, which only attracts more lack and limitation into our lives. It's like this never-ending cycle, and we need to break free from it.

So, how do we do that? Well, the first step is shifting our perspective. Instead of seeing life as some kind of competition where there's only so much to go around, we need to believe deep down that abundance is our birthright. Seriously, the universe is abundant! There's more than enough to fulfill our desires, we just have to open ourselves up to it.

One way to shift our focus from lack to abundance is by practicing gratitude. I know, it sounds cheesy, but trust me on this one. By consciously appreciating what we already have, we're telling the universe that we're open to receiving more. So, take a few moments each day to really feel grateful for the roof over your head, the food on your plate, and the people in your life who bring you joy. It's these little things that pave the way for more abundance to flow in.

But let's not stop there. We've got to reprogram our subconscious mind and replace those scarcity thoughts with thoughts of abundance. That's where affirmations come in. Think of affirmations as these powerful little messages you repeat to yourself every day, reminding yourself of the reality you want to create. So, instead of saying "I never have enough money," reframe it to "I am a magnet for financial abundance." Say these affirmations out loud, and really feel the emotions associated with them as if they've already come true. This is how we shift our energy from scarcity to abundance.

Now, here's where it gets fun - visualization. You've got to create a detailed mental image of your desired reality. So, take some time every day to really picture yourself living a life of abundance. Imagine yourself surrounded by wealth, joy, and endless opportunities. Feel the excitement, the gratitude, and the fulfillment that comes with it. When you consistently visualize abundance, you're aligning your energy with the frequency of abundance and attracting it into your life.

But hey, let's not forget about our physical space. Surrounding ourselves with symbols of abundance can really help shift our mindset. Fill your space with objects that remind you of prosperity and wealth. Maybe it's a vision board with images of your goals, or a jar filled with money, or even a beautiful piece of art that just ignites those feelings of abundance. These visual cues serve as constant reminders of the abundant reality you're creating.

Alright, so we've shifted our thoughts, created these visualizations, and decked out our space with abundance. Now what? It's time for some inspired action, my friend. Manifestation is a co-creative process, which means we got to align our thoughts and intentions with purposeful action. Trust your intuition and take steps that are in line with your desires. By taking action from a place of abundance, you're sending a clear signal to the universe that you're ready to receive all that goodness.

Now, here's the final step - release attachment. Yeah, I know this one can be a toughie, but hear me out. Being super attached to a specific outcome can create resistance and actually block abundance from flowing into our lives. So, practice surrendering to the universe and trust that it knows what's best for you. Let go of that need to control every little thing and have faith in the whole manifestation process. When we loosen our grip on what we think we need, we open ourselves up to receiving even more than we could have ever imagined.

And there you have it! Overcoming scarcity mentality is this transformative journey that requires us to shift our mindset and truly believe in the abundance that's available to us all. By replacing scarcity thoughts with thoughts of abundance, our energy becomes aligned with prosperity, and we start attracting more and more abundance into our lives. Remember, manifestation is a lifelong journey, and as we continue to embrace thoughts of abundance, we open ourselves up to infinite possibilities. So, go ahead and embrace that limitless potential within you, and watch as your reality unfolds in the most beautiful and abundant ways.

Cultivating Gratitude for Abundance

So, here I am, on this wild ride of manifestation. And let me tell you, one thing I've learned really quick is that gratitude is absolutely key. I mean, seriously, it's like the secret ingredient that sets the whole manifestation machine in motion. The more we appreciate and acknowledge the abundance we already have in our lives, the more abundance we attract. It's like a cosmic boomerang, you know? And let me tell you, integrating gratitude into our daily lives can seriously turbocharge our ability to create the life we've always dreamed of.

But listen up, practicing gratitude is no small feat. It's not just about saying a half-hearted "thank you" and calling it a day. No, no. It's about cultivating a whole mindset, a way of being those seeps into every nook and cranny of our existence. It's about really, truly recognizing and cherishing every little blessing that comes our way, big or small. And when we shift our perspective like that, babe, we open ourselves up to a world of infinite possibilities. The Universe becomes our personal genie, ready to grant our every wish.

So, let me drop some gems on how to cultivate that attitude of gratitude. Number one, get yourself a gratitude journal. And I ain't talking about no fluffy diary where you jot down cute little quotes. Nah, this is the real deal. Every day, take a few moments to write down three things you're grateful for. And girl, it can be anything. From a breathtaking sunrise to a soul-warming cup of tea on a chilly morning. By actively acknowledging and appreciating these blessings, you're sending a cosmic message that you're open and ready to receive abundance in all its glory.

Now, let's talk meditation, my friend. Find a cozy spot where you won't hear a peep and get into that zen mode. Focus on your breath, in and out, and start counting your blessings. Picture them in your mind's eye, feel the warmth of gratitude flowing through your entire being. Imagine yourself surrounded by abundance, ready to embrace it with open arms. This practice not only hones our gratitude game, but it deepens our connection with the Universe, priming us for some serious manifestation action.

Nature, darling, she's got something special in store for us too. Take a stroll in the park, or anywhere out in the wild. Chuck out all distractions and be present. Breathe in that crisp air, listen to the sweet melodies of birdsong, and soak in the exquisite details of Mother Nature's masterpiece. With every step, pour out your heart in gratitude for the abundance of nature, and relish the fact that you're just a small part of this grand tapestry. Feel the energy of the Earth under your feet, knowing that you're tapped into an unlimited source of abundance.

But wait, there's more! Affirmations, baby. They're like power pills for reprogramming our subconscious. Sprinkle some gratitude onto your affirmations to really crank up that abundance dial. Say things like, "I'm grateful for all the abundance flowing into my life," or "I'm immensely thankful for the blessings surrounding me." These positive statements declare to the Universe that you're ready and willing to receive even more abundance. And trust me, babe, it's all comin' your way.

Now, this next one is where the magic gets real. Acts of kindness, my love. They go hand in hand with gratitude. There's no better way to cultivate that grateful heart than by lending a hand to those in need. Share your abundance with the less fortunate, offer up your time and skills, or simply lend an ear to someone who needs it. By giving, you're not only expressing gratitude for what you have, but you're also creating a ripple effect of positivity and abundance. It's like the more you give, the more abundance flows right back attach.

And finally, we've got gratitude rituals. Create some special moments throughout your day to really anchor that mindset of abundance. Before every meal, take a second to thank the universe for the nourishment that's about to grace your lips. Like, really feel that gratitude in your soul. And when the morning sun peeks through your window, say a prayer of thanks for the new day and the endless possibilities it holds. These rituals act as little reminders to keep that gratitude flowing strong, and before you know it, it becomes a natural part of who you are.

As you start incorporating these practices into your everyday life, you'll begin to notice a major shift in your core mindset. Gratitude will be your default setting, babe, and abundance will just flow effortlessly into your life. See, it's impossible to bring in more when you're not even grateful for what you already have. So, switch up that perspective, focus on the good stuff, and watch the Universe respond in the most mind-blowing ways.

In a nutshell, cultivating gratitude for abundance is like rocket fuel for your manifestation journey. Once you start acknowledging and appreciating the blessings already in your life, brace yourself, babe. The floodgates of abundance are about to burst wide open. So, make a promise to yourself, commit to this mindset of gratitude, and witness the Universe shower you with blessings beyond your wildest dreams. Embrace the power of gratitude, my friend, and let it guide you straight to the life you've always craved.

Embracing the Law of Circulation

You know what's funny? The more I dive into the law of attraction, the more I realize that the universe is like this wild, constantly moving and shifting force that's responding to every thought and belief we have. It's like this invisible magnet that's aligning everything and everyone to give us what we want. But here's the thing, just thinking about what we desire isn't enough. We gotta embody the feeling of already having it. It's like tricking the universe into thinking our desires have already happened. And when we do that, the universe is like, "Alright, let's make it happen!"

I've learned that the key to unlocking the power of manifestation is to focus on what we want, rather than getting caught up in what we don't have. We gotta tap into that abundance mindset and trust that the universe has our back. Manifestation isn't bound by time, you know? If we truly believe and align our thoughts and feelings with our desires, boom, it can happen like magic. Start small, like little wins here and there, and watch how it builds up our confidence to attract bigger and better things.

Here's a cool technique I've been using: creating my day in advance. It's like prepping ourselves to live out the reality we want. By consciously thinking about how we want our day to go, we're setting the stage for our manifestation journey. It's crazy how our circumstances are just a reflection of the thoughts we've been chewing on. But hey, we have the power to change that by shifting our thoughts and feelings. It's all about being aware of what vibes we're putting out there because like attracts like. We're legit magnets, attracting everything based on our thoughts and emotions. So, let's direct our thoughts and feelings toward what we actually want, and watch it effortlessly come into our lives.

Now, trust, my friend, trust is a biggie in this manifestation game. The universe has its own timing, you know? We gotta believe that everything will unfold step by step. Declare our desires to the universe and truly, wholeheartedly believe that we're receiving them. It's like putting out an order to the universe and being like, "You, I know you got my back and I trust that you'll bring it to me when the time is right." And here's the thing about prosperity, think about that instead of focusing on debt. Let's shift our perspective and appreciate what we have right now, creating a vibrational frequency that attracts abundance.

Look, life isn't all rainbows and butterflies, we both know that. But the key is to find a way to feel good despite the challenges. By directing our attention towards the good stuff and focusing away from the difficulties, we're inviting more of that goodness in. Energy flows where attention goes, so let's focus on what we wanna experience, rather than what we wanna avoid.

Embracing the Law of Circulation, my friend, that's a biggie too. It's all about celebrating the world as it is, going with the flow of the universe. When we fully accept and appreciate the present, we align ourselves with the natural flow of abundance. We gotta take responsibility for our thoughts, let go of the stuff we don't want, and release any resistance. We're the masters of our lives, after all.

To manifest our desires, we gotta believe deep down that we've already received them. It's all about feeling those emotions associated with our desires and energetically aligning ourselves with their manifestation. We're literally turning our wildest fantasies into reality, and that opens up space for even bigger dreams. Our belief in our desires coming true sets the stage for their fulfillment.

And let's not forget about action, my friend. Taking inspired action that feels good and aligned with the universe is a must in this whole manifestation process. It's about aligning our thoughts, beliefs, and our external actions. When we take inspired action, we're co-creating with the abundant flow of the universe, making our desires manifest effortlessly.

Here's the thing, when we truly grasp the Law of Circulation, we open ourselves up to a whole world of possibilities. We see that giving and receiving go hand in hand. It's like this circular flow of energy, thoughts, and intentions, and we get to participate in it consciously. We have the power to shape our reality, my friend. We have the power to live a life of limitless abundance and fulfillment.

Chapter 15: Putting Manifestation into Action

Creating a Personalized Manifestation Plan

Creating a Personalized Manifestation Plan is an essential step towards harnessing the ultimate power of manifestation. It is the roadmap that guides us towards achieving our desires and goals. Without a clear and personalized plan, the manifestation process can become hazy and unattainable. In this chapter, we will delve into the importance of having a personalized manifestation plan and explore the concept of manifesting desires and goals.

Manifestation is a powerful process that allows us to transform our thoughts and intentions into reality. It involves aligning our thoughts, beliefs, and actions with the desired outcome. Understanding the intricacies of manifestation and how it works is crucial in order to effectively manifest our desires. By setting clear intentions, we are able to direct our energy towards what we truly want, increasing the likelihood of success.

Identifying and clarifying our personal desires and goals is a fundamental step in the manifestation process. It requires self-reflection and deep introspection to uncover our true desires. Through brainstorming and journaling, we can gain clarity on what truly matters to us. This self-exploration enables us to align our desires with our values and beliefs, making our manifestation plan more authentic and powerful.

One powerful tool that aids in the manifestation process is the creation of a vision board. A vision board serves as a visual representation of our desires and goals. By using images, words, and symbols that resonate with us, we are able to amplify our intentions and increase our focus on what we want to manifest. In this chapter, I will provide step-by-step instructions on how to create a vision board that will serve as a powerful manifestation tool.

Breaking down larger goals into smaller, achievable action steps is a key strategy in successful manifestation. By doing so, we make our goals more manageable and less overwhelming. In this chapter, I will guide you on how to identify and prioritize action steps for each goal, enabling you to take consistent and intentional action towards your desires.

Tracking our progress is crucial in the manifestation journey. It allows us to celebrate our successes and make necessary adjustments to our plan. I will share various methods and tools that can be used to track progress, such as journaling or using apps, ensuring that we stay on track and maintain momentum.

Implementing daily practices that support manifestation is another crucial aspect of our personalized plan. By incorporating specific daily practices, such as gratitude exercises or visualization techniques, we enhance our focus and energy towards our desires. These practices serve as powerful reminders and reinforce our belief in the manifestation process.

Challenges and limiting beliefs are common obstacles that may arise during the manifestation process. In this chapter, I will discuss these challenges and provide guidance on how to overcome them. By identifying and addressing these roadblocks, we can ensure that they do not hinder our progress towards manifesting our desires.

Staying motivated and focused is vital in successfully manifesting our desires. I will share tips and strategies that can help us stay motivated and committed to our manifestation plan. Additionally, I will explore the importance of incorporating accountability and support systems to ensure that we stay on track and maintain our momentum.

Regularly reviewing and revising our manifestation plan is an integral part of the process. By evaluating our progress and making necessary adjustments, we ensure that our plan remains aligned with our desires. In this chapter, I will provide guidance on how to review and revise our manifestation plan, ensuring that it continues to support our journey towards manifestation.

By creating a personalized manifestation plan, we are harnessing the ultimate power of manifestation. Through understanding the process, setting clear intentions, identifying desires and goals, creating a vision board, breaking down goals into action steps, tracking progress, implementing daily practices, overcoming challenges and limiting beliefs, staying motivated and focused, and regularly reviewing and revising our plan, we are well-equipped to manifest our desires and achieve our goals. The power lies within us to manifest the life we truly desire.

Daily Practices to Keep Your Manifestation Journey on Track

Maintaining focus and momentum on the manifestation journey is crucial for achieving desired outcomes. Daily practices play a significant role in this process by providing a structured framework that helps individuals stay on track and align their thoughts, beliefs, and actions with their intentions. In this subchapter, we will explore the importance of incorporating daily practices into our manifestation journey and introduce various practices that can support us along the way.

Morning Rituals for Manifestation

The way we start our day sets the tone for everything that follows. By incorporating morning rituals into our daily routine, we can infuse our mornings with intention and positivity, allowing us to approach each day with clarity and purpose. One of the most powerful morning rituals for manifestation is meditation. Taking a few moments to sit in stillness, quieting the mind and connecting with our inner selves, can help us align our energy and set a positive intention for the day ahead.

Another morning ritual that can support manifestation is journaling. By putting our thoughts and feelings onto paper, we create space for self-reflection and gain a deeper understanding of our desires and intentions. Setting intentions is another powerful morning ritual that can help us focus our energy and attention on what we want to manifest. By consciously stating our desires and affirming our commitment to their realization, we create a powerful foundation for manifestation.

Visualization Exercises for Manifestation

Visualization is a powerful tool for manifesting our desires. It involves using our imagination to create detailed mental images of what we want to attract into our lives. Visualization exercises can range from creating vision boards to guided visualizations and mental rehearsals. By consistently visualizing our desired outcomes, we align our thoughts, beliefs, and emotions with what we want to manifest, making it more likely to become our reality.

Affirmation Practices for Manifestation

Affirmations are positive statements that affirm our desired outcomes. By repeating these affirmations daily, we reprogram our subconscious mind and replace limiting beliefs with empowering ones. Daily affirmations, affirmations in front of a mirror, and writing affirmations are different practices that can be incorporated into our manifestation journey. Affirmations help us cultivate a positive mindset, increase our self-belief, and strengthen our alignment with our desires.

Gratitude Rituals for Manifestation

Gratitude plays a vital role in the manifestation process. By focusing on what we are grateful for, we shift our perspective towards abundance and positivity, attracting more of what we appreciate into our lives. Gratitude rituals such as gratitude journaling, gratitude prayers, and gratitude walks can deepen our sense of appreciation and enhance our manifestation journey. These rituals remind us to celebrate the small victories and acknowledge the abundance already present in our lives.

Combining Daily Practices for Maximum Effectiveness

By combining different daily practices, we can amplify the effectiveness of our manifestation journey. Each practice complements and enhances the others, creating a synergistic effect. For example, starting the day with a morning ritual sets a positive tone for the day, while incorporating visualization and affirmation practices throughout the day reinforces our intentions and beliefs. By experimenting with different combinations of practices, we can find a routine that resonates with us and supports our manifestation process.

Tailoring Daily Practices to Individual Needs

Personalizing daily practices is essential for their effectiveness. It is important to choose practices that resonate with our individual preferences and beliefs. For example, if meditation is not appealing, we can explore other mindfulness practices that suit us better.

Additionally, we should adapt and modify practices to fit specific circumstances or limitations. By tailoring daily practices to our unique needs, we ensure that they are sustainable and aligned with our authentic selves.

Staying Consistent and Committed to Daily Practices

Maintaining consistency in daily practices can be challenging, but it is crucial for long-term success in manifestation. It requires dedication and perseverance, especially when faced with obstacles or distractions. To stay committed, it is helpful to develop strategies and implement tips such as creating accountability systems, setting reminders, and finding support networks. By prioritizing daily practices and making them a non-negotiable part of our routine, we increase our chances of manifesting our desires.

Tracking Progress and Adjusting Daily Practices

Tracking progress in daily practices is essential for evaluating their effectiveness and making adjustments if necessary. By monitoring our experiences and outcomes, we can assess which practices are yielding the desired results and which may need to be modified or replaced. Using tools or methods such as journaling, reflection, or even seeking guidance from mentors or coaches can provide valuable insights and help us refine our daily practices.

Conclusion and Encouragement

In conclusion, daily practices are an integral part of the manifestation journey. They provide structure, focus, and momentum, helping us align our thoughts, beliefs, and actions with our desires. By implementing morning rituals, visualization exercises, affirmation practices, gratitude rituals, and combining them strategically, we can maximize the effectiveness of our manifestation journey. It is important to tailor these practices to our individual needs, stay consistent and committed, track progress, and make necessary adjustments along the way. So, dear readers, I encourage you to start implementing and experimenting with these practices. Embrace the potential transformation and fulfillment that consistent daily practices can bring into your life. The power of manifestation is within your grasp, and with dedication and perseverance, you can manifest the life of your dreams.

Cultivating Patience and Trust in the Process

Patience and trust are two fundamental qualities that play a vital role in the manifestation process. As individuals embark on their journey of manifesting their desires, it is crucial for them to understand the importance of cultivating patience and trust. These qualities serve as guiding forces, helping individuals stay focused, positive, and resilient throughout the manifestation journey.

The Power of Patience:

Patience is more than just waiting for things to happen; it is a mindset that allows individuals to maintain their composure and inner peace, even in the face of uncertainty. In the realm of manifestation, patience is crucial because it helps individuals avoid the trap of impatience, which can hinder progress and create resistance. When we are impatient, we often try to force outcomes and control the timing of our desires, which can be counterproductive.

To cultivate patience, individuals can engage in mindfulness practices that allow them to stay present and grounded. By focusing on the present moment, they can release attachment to the future and cultivate a sense of peace. Reframing expectations is another technique for cultivating patience. Rather than fixating on a specific timeline, individuals can shift their focus to the process itself, embracing each step as part of the journey.

Surrendering to the Timing of the Universe:

Surrendering to the timing of the universe is an essential aspect of the manifestation process. When we try to control the timing, we often create stress and limit our ability to manifest our desires. By surrendering, we let go of the need for immediate results and trust that the universe has a perfect timing for everything.

To surrender, individuals can practice letting go of attachment. This means releasing the grip on desired outcomes and accepting that they may manifest in a different form or at a different time than initially envisioned. Acceptance is another powerful technique for surrendering. By embracing what is and acknowledging that everything is unfolding as it should, individuals can release resistance and open themselves up to greater possibilities.

Trusting the Journey:

Trusting the journey is vital for maintaining a positive mindset and staying aligned with our desires, even when faced with obstacles or setbacks. When we trust the process, we remain confident that everything is working in our favor and that our desires are manifesting, even if it may not be immediately apparent.

To cultivate trust, individuals can engage in daily affirmations that reinforce their belief in the manifestation power. By repeating positive statements such as "I trust the process," individuals program their subconscious mind to align with their desires. Visualization is another powerful technique for cultivating trust. By vividly imagining the fulfillment of their desires, individuals strengthen their belief in the manifestation process and reinforce their trust in the journey.

The Unexpected Twists of Manifestation:

Manifestation is not always a linear path; it often involves unexpected twists and turns. These twists can be opportunities for growth and learning. Patience and trust play a crucial role in navigating these twists, allowing individuals to adapt and adjust their approach without losing sight of their desires.

Embracing Uncertainty:

Uncertainty is an inherent part of the manifestation process. It is natural to feel uncertain or even fearful when stepping into the unknown. However, cultivating patience and trust can help individuals embrace uncertainty and stay open to new possibilities.

To embrace uncertainty, individuals can practice surrendering to the unknown. This involves releasing the need for certainty and control, and instead, surrendering to the flow of life. Gratitude practices can also help individuals embrace uncertainty by shifting their focus to what is already present and abundant in their lives.

Overcoming Impatience and Doubt:

Impatience and doubt are common challenges that can arise during the manifestation process. However, with patience and trust, individuals can overcome these challenges and stay committed to their desires.

Affirmations are a powerful tool for overcoming impatience and doubt. By repeating positive statements such as "I am patient and trust the process," individuals rewire their thought patterns and reinforce their belief in the manifestation process. Self-reflection is another technique that can help individuals overcome these challenges. By examining the root causes of impatience and doubt, individuals can gain insights and develop strategies to overcome them.

Learning from Delayed Manifestations:

Delayed manifestations can be disheartening, but they also offer valuable insights and lessons. Patience and trust are crucial in navigating disappointment and maintaining a positive outlook.

Journaling is an effective technique for learning from delayed manifestations. By writing down their thoughts, feelings, and observations, individuals can gain clarity and uncover hidden patterns or beliefs that may be hindering their manifestation journey. Seeking support from mentors or like-minded individuals can also provide valuable guidance and encouragement during times of delay.

Staying Aligned with Desires:

Patience and trust are key to staying aligned with our desires. Impatience and doubt can create resistance and hinder the manifestation process, making it essential to cultivate these qualities.

Visualization is a powerful technique for staying aligned with desires. By vividly imagining the fulfillment of their desires, individuals strengthen their focus and belief in the manifestation process. Affirmations can also help individuals stay aligned by reinforcing positive beliefs and intentions.

Celebrating the Journey:

Celebrating small victories and milestones during the manifestation process is vital for boosting motivation and reinforcing the belief in the manifestation power. By acknowledging and appreciating progress, individuals cultivate a sense of gratitude and optimism.

Gratitude practices, such as daily gratitude journaling or expressing gratitude towards oneself, can help individuals celebrate the journey. Self-care is another technique that can enhance the celebration experience. Engaging in activities that bring joy and relaxation, individuals honor themselves and the progress they have made.

In conclusion, patience and trust are essential qualities that can greatly enhance the manifestation process. By cultivating these qualities, individuals can stay focused, positive, and resilient, even in the face of challenges and unexpected twists. Through techniques such as mindfulness, surrendering, affirmations, and visualization, individuals can harness the power of patience and trust to manifest their desires and create the life they truly desire.

Celebrating and Acknowledging Manifestations

As I sit here reflecting on the power of manifestation, I can't help but be in awe of the incredible journey it has taken me on. The concept of celebrating and acknowledging manifestations has been a crucial aspect of my own path, and it is one that I am eager to share with others.

Manifestations, at their core, represent the realization of our deepest desires and goals. Whether it be material wealth, personal relationships, or spiritual growth, manifestations serve as a tangible reminder that the universe is constantly working in our favor. This idea is deeply intertwined with the broader theme of manifestation and the law of attraction, as we are encouraged to align our thoughts and energy with what we want to attract into our lives.

But where did these practices of celebrating and acknowledging manifestations originate? It is fascinating to explore the historical and social context in which these rituals and practices have emerged. Different cultures and traditions have long recognized the power of manifestation, and they have developed unique ways of celebrating and acknowledging it. From ancient civilizations to modern societies, the celebration of manifestations has been a common thread throughout history.

Cultural analysis of manifestation rituals reveals a diverse array of practices used to honor and give thanks for manifested desires. Gratitude ceremonies, prayer, and offerings to deities are just a few examples of these rituals. Each one carries deep symbolism and significance, offering a profound connection between the individual and the divine forces at play.

Beyond cultural rituals, individuals have their own personal practices to celebrate and acknowledge manifestations. Journaling, visualization, and creating vision boards are just a few examples of these practices. Engaging in these activities not only helps to maintain a positive mindset but also amplifies the energy for future manifestations. It is through these practices that we can truly harness the power of manifestation.

One vital aspect of celebrating manifestations is the role of gratitude. Expressing gratitude for the desires that have already manifested in our lives is an essential part of the manifestation process. By acknowledging and appreciating what we have, we create an open space for even more abundance to flow into our lives. Keeping a gratitude journal or practicing daily affirmations are powerful ways to cultivate a grateful mindset.

Comparing manifestation celebrations across different cultures reveals intriguing insights into the impact of cultural context on these practices. Rituals, practices, and beliefs surrounding manifestations vary greatly, yet they all share the common goal of celebrating and acknowledging the power of manifestation. It is through these cultural differences that we can gain a deeper understanding of the universal principles at work.

The power of community in manifestation celebrations cannot be underestimated. Sharing our manifestations with others amplifies the positive energy and reinforces our belief in the manifestation process. Communal rituals and gatherings centered around celebrating manifestations create a powerful sense of unity and support among like-minded individuals.

The intersection of spirituality and manifestation celebrations is a profound aspect to explore. Different spiritual beliefs and practices influence the manifestation rituals we engage in. Whether it be through meditation, prayer, or connecting with our higher selves, spirituality plays a crucial role in our manifestation journey. It is through this connection that we can tap into the infinite potential within us.

The psychological effects of celebrating manifestations are undeniable. By acknowledging our achievements, we boost our self-confidence and motivation to continue on our manifestation journey. Positive reinforcement through celebration has a profound impact on our future manifestation efforts, encouraging us to keep moving forward with unwavering belief in the power of manifestation.

In conclusion, celebrating and acknowledging manifestations is a crucial aspect of the manifestation process. By incorporating celebration and gratitude practices into our daily lives, we tap into the limitless power within us and align ourselves with the universe's abundant energy. So, I invite you to join me on this incredible journey of manifestation and embrace the power of celebration and gratitude. Let us honor our manifestations, big and small, and witness the magic that unfolds as we celebrate our desires coming to life.

Chapter 16: Unleashing Creativity for Manifestation

Vision Board Collage

Step 1: Clarify Your Desires

So, before we dive into creating this epic vision board collage, we gotta get super clear on what we actually want, okay? Take a moment and really think about what you want to bring into your life. Is it buckets of cash, an amazing partnership, being a total health queen, or crushing it in your career? Whatever it is, get specific. Visualize those desires like they're playing on a 4K Ultra HD screen and really feel 'em in your bones. The clearer you are on what you want, the better we can put together a board that screams "this is my destiny!"

Step 2: Gather Materials

Alright, let's gather our materials like we're about to rock an arts and crafts session in kindergarten. Get yourself a big old' poster board or just a really large piece of paper - we're talking big enough to handle all your dreams. Next, raid your house for magazines, newspapers, and anything else that has juicy images and words that give you those "heck yeah, that's what I want" vibes. Don't forget, you can also throw in some personal photos, inspirational quotes, and symbols that are totally meaningful to you. And please, please, have scissors and glue or tape on standby. We're about to get sticky.

Step 3: Select Images

Time to unleash your inner Sherlock Holmes and start digging into those magazines. Flip through the pages and trust your gut. If an image or word grabs your attention like a pop-up ad, then snip it out and put it in the "heck yeah, I love this" pile. Look for visuals that get you pumped up, that spark that fire inside you. Trust me, your intuition knows what it's doing. Cut those babies out and set them aside - we're about to turn 'em into magic.

Step 4: Arrange and Organize

Alright, now the real fun begins. We've got our images, words, and a big blank canvas in front of us. Some people like to get all organized and structured, dividing their board into sections for different areas of life. You know, like career, relationships, health, and all that jazz. Others like to go with the flow and just let their creativity take the wheel. Do whatever floats your boat, my friend. Start arranging your images on the board, like you're putting together the pieces of a puzzle. Let your imagination run wild and have a dance party with your creativity.

Step 5: Infuse with Intention

Now, here's where the real magic happens. As you place each image or word on your board, take a moment to really feel into it. Visualize yourself already living out those desires. Feel the excitement, the joy, the relief, the success - all of it. As you attach each image, mentally connect with it and send your intention right into it. You can even say some positive affirmations or declarations that match your desires. This is like giving your vision board a supercharged shot of manifestation energy. Boom!

Step 6: Personalization and Creativity

This is your vision board, so let's make sure it screams "you!" Add some personal touches, my friend. Throw in some photos of yourself, your loved ones, or even that adorable kitten you saw on the internet (hey, no judgment here). Grab a pen and write some heartfelt letters expressing your gratitude or affirmations. You can even sprinkle in some objects that hold symbolic meaning for you. Let it all reflect who you are and what you're all about. This board is gonna be your BFF for manifesting, so make it shines like a diamond.

Step 7: Display and Review

Time to find your vision board its new forever home. Find a spot where it can be the star of the show, like your bedroom wall or your office space. Somewhere you'll see it every day, multiple times a day. Let it catch your eye like a sparkling disco ball. Take a few minutes each day to really soak it all in, my friend. Look at those images and visualize your desires as if they're already here. Feel the freaking joy and gratitude coursing through your veins. This is how you keep your dreams front and center, reminding yourself that they're oh-so-possible.

Step 8: Take Inspired Action

Alright, here comes the real sizzle. While creating this vision board is like throwing a mega party for your subconscious, it's not gonna magically poof your desires into existence. Nope, you gotta back it up with some action, my friend. This vision board is gonna light a fire under your booty to start taking inspired action. Look at it as your personal compass, pointing you in the right direction. Whether it's making bold moves with your finances, adopting healthier habits, or connecting with folks in your industry, let this board be your guide. Take those steps towards your dreams like a boss.

In conclusion, creating a vision board collage is like summoning the dream squad for your manifesting game. It helps you physically see your desires and reminds you to go after them with all you've got. By choosing images that make your heart race and infusing them with intention, you tap into the power of your thoughts and become a manifestation maven. So, embrace this incredible journey of making your dreams come true and remember, my friend, you've got the power within you to create the life you've always dreamed of. Now go out there and show the universe what you're made of!

Artistic Expression for Manifestation

You know, I've always believed that artistic expression is like this secret superpower we all possess. It's this incredible tool that allows us to bring our thoughts and dreams into the physical world. I mean, how cool is that? Whether it's painting, drawing, or sculpting, art gives us this unique way to manifest our desires.

But here's the thing: picking the right medium is everything. Some folks find their zen in painting, where they can splash colors and blend brushstrokes to create a vivid picture of their desires. Others prefer the precision of drawing, where they can meticulously bring their visions to life on paper. And then there are those who find solace in sculpting, and they get to mold and shape their dreams with their own hands. It's like finding the perfect outlet for your creative energy, you know?

Now, once you've settled on your chosen medium, it's time to infuse your artwork with intention. And trust me, intention is everything. You've gotta be mindful and intentional about what you want your art to manifest. So, take a moment, reflect on your desires, and set some clear intentions. What do you want to bring into your life? What do you want to let go of? Answering these questions will give your artwork that energy and intention it needs to make it all happen.

And don't forget about symbolism. Yeah, symbols are like these secret messages we can slip into our art to amplify our intentions. Every object, color, and shape have its own meaning, its own little superpower. So why not sprinkle them into your artwork? If you're after financial abundance, throw in a gold coin or a money tree. Want love and a soulmate? How about a heart or intertwined hands? You get the idea. Symbols are like this secret code that speaks directly to the universe and attracts the energy you want.

Now, brace yourself, because as you create your masterpiece, you've gotta stay connected to the emotions and feelings linked to your desires. Art has this incredible ability to stir up emotions and forge a deep connection with what we want. So let those emotions guide you, let them dance with your brushstrokes or pencil lines. Whether it's joy, love, or gratitude, let those feelings infuse your artwork with the kind of vibrant energy that'll make your desires come alive.

And while we're at it, let's not forget to infuse your art with a little bit of your own energy too. Your art is an extension of you, my friend. It's this beautiful reflection of your inner self. So let it all out. Pour your thoughts, emotions, and experiences into your artwork. Let it be a testament to your journey and the growth that you've experienced. By weaving your energy into your art, you're creating this magnetic force field that'll draw your desires straight to you.

Oh, and a couple more things. When you're creating your art specifically for manifestation, make sure you're in a calm and focused environment. Find a space that inspires you and banish any distractions. This is like your creative sanctuary, so make it perfect. And hey, remember to stay mindful and present. Be in the moment as you create, and don't let your mind wander. It's in those precious moments of being fully present that you'll infuse your art with that magic manifestation energy.

And lastly, my friend, trust the process. This whole manifestation thing through art isn't about forcing outcomes or trying to control the end result. No, it's about surrendering to the creative process and letting the universe work its magic. So, trust that your art is gonna bring your desires to life in the most perfect way, at just the right time.

So, to sum it all up, artistic expression is like this divine superpower. Through painting, drawing, and sculpting, we can tap into our creativity and bring our dreams into reality. It's our bridge between thoughts and intentions and the beautiful world of manifestation. So, grab that paintbrush, sketch that pencil, or get your hands dirty with clay. Let your art be the magic key that unlocks your dreams and watch as your desires manifest right before your eyes. It's gonna be epic.

Creative Visualization Techniques

Creative visualization. It's like having a superpower, a secret weapon that allows you to make your dreams a reality. Picture this: you close your eyes and let your imagination run wild. You see it with such clarity, as if it's right in front of you. But it's not just pictures in your head; it's a whole experience. You can hear the sounds, smell the scents, feel the textures, taste the flavors. You're fully immersed in this vibrant mental world that you've created.

Now, in the world of manifestation, visualization isn't some new-age gimmick. It's been around for ages, recognized and used by spiritual and philosophical traditions across time. They've always known that the mind is a powerful thing, capable of shaping our reality. And creative visualization is the key to unlocking that power within you.

So, how do you harness this power? Let me share some techniques that'll help you become a master of the art. First, it's not just about seeing things in your mind's eye. It's about engaging all your senses. Close your eyes, yes, but also listen, smell, touch, taste. Make it a multi-dimensional experience, like living in a different world.

And to get into the visualization zone, create a sacred space. Find a quiet corner where you can escape the distractions of everyday life. Decorate it with symbols and colors that speak to your desires. This is your personal sanctuary, where you can dive deep into your imagination.

If you're new to visualization or find it a challenge, guided sessions can be a game-changer. There are plenty of recordings and videos that'll take you on a journey through your mind. Let them guide you, give you cues and imagery that'll help you picture exactly what you want.

Now, here's one of my favorite techniques: the vision board. Think of it as your dreams on a poster. This physical representation of your desires keeps them alive and fresh in your mind. Just give it a glance, and you'll instantly be back in that mental space, ready to manifest your dreams.

And speaking of manifesting, try this technique: role-playing. Pretend you're already living that dream life. Picture yourself confidently achieving your goals, experiencing the joy and fulfillment that come with it. Be that future version of yourself, and let it shape your actions and thoughts.

Writing is a powerful tool for manifestation, too. Use your journal to describe your dreams in vivid detail. Paint a picture with your words, capturing all the sights, sounds, and emotions. This process solidifies your intentions and gives you a record you can come back to whenever you need a boost.

Now, let's take it up a notch with storytelling. Imagine yourself as the hero of your own adventure. Tell the tale of how you conquered obstacles and achieved your dreams. Really immerse yourself in the experience, feel the triumphs, and embrace the transformations.

Combine all these techniques with meditation, and boom – you've got a recipe for success. Take a moment to create that mental image of your desires, and hold onto it as you meditate. Let it come to life, becoming more vibrant and detailed with each breath. Feel the energy, the emotions, aligning with the reality you wish to create.

This is the power of creative visualization. By engaging your mind and senses, you're activating the law of attraction. You become a magnet, drawing in the experiences, people, and circumstances needed to manifest your goals. But remember, this isn't a one-time thing. It's a lifelong journey of consistency, belief, and unwavering focus on your dreams. Integrate these techniques into your daily life, make them a part of who you are.

With creative visualization, you have the power to manifest your wildest dreams. It's transformative, allowing you to tap into your unlimited potential and create a life of abundance, joy, and fulfillment. So, embrace this art, unleash your manifesting power, and let your dreams become your reality.

Chapter 17: Advanced Manifestation Techniques

Quantum Manifestation

So here we are, diving deeper into the realm of manifestation and getting all tangled up with quantum physics. I know, it sounds fancy and complicated, but stick with me. Quantum physics is like the CSI of science, trying to crack the case of reality at its smallest, tiniest level – the atomic and subatomic level. It's a world where particles can be in multiple states all at once and can even change just by being observed. Mind-blowing, right?

In this chapter, we're getting into the nitty-gritty of how these quantum mechanics principles can actually be applied to our manifesting game. We're talking about how our thoughts, beliefs, and intentions interact with this quantum field thingamajig, and how we can use it to bring our desires to life faster and smoother than ever.

1. The Quantum Field

Let's start with the basics. Picture this – the quantum field is this vast, interconnected spiderweb of energy that covers the whole universe. It's not just the stuff that makes up everything in existence, but also this playground of infinite possibilities. It's like our desires are little boats bobbing up and down in that quantum sea, just waiting to be brought to shore. By understanding the rules of this field and how it jives with our minds, we can sail our manifesting ship with precision and clarity.

2. The Observer Effect

Alright, imagine this – in quantum physics, there's this thing called the observer effect. Basically, when you actually look at a particle or a system, it suddenly decides to get its act together and take on a specific state or position. Yeah, just by being observed, it changes. Crazy, right?

Now, think about this in terms of manifestation. It shows us that what we focus on and what we truly believe has the power to collapse all those possibilities in the quantum field and make our desires pop into our physical reality. So, our attention and belief in the manifestation process are like little magic wands, shaping the outcome of what we want.

3. Entanglement

Here's something juicy – quantum physics introduces this concept called entanglement. When two particles become entangled, their properties become linked up, no matter how far apart they are. It's like there's some secret connection that ties all the things in the universe together. Mind-boggling, am I right?

Now, let's apply this to manifestation. Our desires are entangled with the quantum field, like they're soulmates or something. When we align our thoughts, beliefs, and intentions with what we want, we're creating this epic love story between ourselves and the quantum field. This means we can tap into all the information and resources we need to manifest our desires like it's a piece of cake.

4. Quantum Superposition

Hold onto your hats, folks. Quantum superposition is the idea that particles can exist in multiple states all at once until someone looks at them or measures them. It's like they're playing a game of multiple-choice and only make up their minds when someone picks an answer. Sound crazy? Well, it is.

So, take this wild concept and apply it to manifestation. Our desires can exist in a million different forms and possibilities, just like those particles. This means we gotta dream big, expand our imagination, and be open to the craziest ways our wishes can come true. No limits, baby!

5. Quantum Coherence

Imagine this – quantum coherence is when particles are perfectly aligned and work together like a well-oiled machine. They're all in sync and that's when the magic happens. When particles are in this state, they can make instant, mind-blowing changes. Like poof, now you see it, now you don't.

And guess what? Coherence is the real deal when it comes to manifesting too. When our thoughts, beliefs, and intentions are all in perfect harmony with our desires, it's like we're part of this cosmic symphony. That's when our manifesting power gets cranked up to 11. By keeping that high level of coherence, we can create fast and amazing shifts in our reality.

6. Harnessing Quantum Manifestation

Alright, now that we've got the lowdown on all this quantum stuff, it's time to put it into action. Here's what you gotta do:

a. Make your thoughts and beliefs your BFFs: Just like those particles getting all entangled, we gotta get our thoughts, beliefs, and desires all in perfect harmony. Focus on thoughts that cheer on your manifestations and wave goodbye to any doubts or limiting beliefs trying to spoil the party.

b. Get a little cozy with coherence: Do things that make you feel grounded and in the zone. Meditate, visualize, practice gratitude – whatever gets you humming like a well-tuned engine. Hitting that state of coherence amps up your manifesting skills and gets you partying with the quantum field.

c. Embrace the wild ride: In this quantum world, anything goes. Embrace the uncertainty, let go of the need to control everything. Surrender to the magic and let the quantum field do its thing. Trust that the universe has some kickass surprises up its sleeve for you.

d. Take inspired action: Manifesting is all about teamwork, baby. The universe is your sidekick, but you gotta do your part too. Listen to your gut, trust those vibes, and take action that feels inspired. The quantum field has got your back, trust me.

e. Celebrate those wins: When your desires start popping up in your life, don't forget to throw a little party. Give props to the quantum field for its abundant support and have confidence that more epic manifestations are coming in hot.

Conclusion

Phew, quantum manifestation is like opening up Pandora's box of possibilities. By grasping the principles of quantum physics and working with them, we can dive into the quantum field, turn our dreams into reality, and have a blast co-creating our dream lives.

Always remember, you're the captain of your reality. Your thoughts, beliefs, and intentions have the power to shape your entire experience. So, jump into this exciting world of quantum manifestation and unleash the ultimate power of your mind. The universe is beyond stoked to team up with you and make your wildest dreams come true. Embrace the limitless potential of the quantum field and get ready to watch magic unfold like never before.

Energy Clearing and Alignment

You know, there's this awesome way to clear and align our energy that I've discovered. It's all about working with these incredible energy healers. These folks are like energy masters, they know all the ins and outs of energy flow in our bodies. They use these different healing methods like Reiki, chakra healing, and energy balancing to find any blocked energy and zap it away. It's like opening up a dam and letting all the good energy flow freely. I've found that these blocks can come from past traumas, negative experiences, or just some messed-up beliefs we've picked up along the way. But with the help of these healers, we can say goodbye to those blocks and make way for some seriously positive energy and all the good stuff that comes with it.

Crystals have also become my trusty sidekicks in this energy-clearing journey. I mean, these little guys are like pocket-sized powerhouses. Each crystal has its own unique energy and properties that we can use to balance and align our own energy. Check this out - amethyst is all about calm and purifying vibes, while citrine is like a magnet for abundance and manifestation. So, what I started doing is picking out the right crystals and using them in special ways, like making crystal grids or taking crystal baths. Or sometimes, I'll just carry them around with me all day long, like my own personal cheerleaders for my intentions. It's like they turn up the volume on my manifestations.

But wait, there's more! I've also found some seriously powerful tools that kick up the energy-clearing game. Essential oils have been used forever and a day to bring harmony to the mind, body, and spirit. Each oil has its own vibe, and when I add them into my daily rituals and meditation, it's like they kick out any bad energy and bring in all the good ones. It's like my mood goes from blah to woohoo in no time.

Let's not forget about the ancient art of smudging. Now, this is a game-changer in the energy-clearing biz. Picture this - you burn sacred herbs like sage or palo santo and the smoke wafts around, cleansing and purifying your whole energy field. It's like a total energy spring cleaning. And while I'm smudging, I set the intention to let go of all those pesky blockages and get in sync with my manifestations. It's like hitting the reset button.

Now, let me introduce you to sound healing. This one is a real treat for the senses. Sound has its own magic, you know. Singing bowls, drums, and even specific sound frequencies can totally change the energy game. They shake things up, balance our chakras, and bring this blissful state of relaxation and harmony to our bodies and minds. It's like a sonic massage for the soul.

But here's the thing, my friend - energy clearing and alignment isn't just a one-time thing. It's a lifelong practice. As we grow and change, new blocks and challenges pop up, and we've gotta keep clearing and aligning our energy. So, I've started incorporating these techniques into my daily life, making it part of my routine. Just like brushing my teeth or checking my phone (let's be real), I make sure to take care of and nurture my energy. And let me tell you, it's made a huge difference. My manifestations come to life faster than ever before, big dreams and little wishes alike. It's like I've tapped into this limitless potential and the possibilities are endless.

But hey, I gotta tell you, what works for me might not work for you. Energy clearing and alignment is personal, it's all about what resonates with your heart and soul. So, trust your gut and find the practices that speak to you.

As I reflect on my own journey with energy clearing and alignment, I'm just blown away. This stuff has transformed my life in ways I never thought possible. By releasing those energy blocks and getting in tune with a higher vibration, I've seen my desires manifest before my very eyes. It's like a magic show, except it's my own life being transformed. Taking care of my energy has created this beautiful harmony and empowerment in my life. And the best part? It's never-ending. This manifestation journey is gonna last a lifetime, and energy clearing and alignment are my secret weapons for unlocking my full potential and becoming the best version of myself. So, let's dive in, my friend. Let's clear the way for our wildest dreams to become our everyday reality.

Sacred Geometry and Manifestation

Have you ever wondered about the mysterious world of sacred geometry? It's like this secret language that unlocks the secrets of creation and manifestation. I mean, can you even imagine? It's been studied and revered by ancient civilizations for ages, and now we have the chance to tap into its power ourselves.

Picture this: a symphony of shapes and patterns, dancing and intertwining to form the very fabric of the universe. That's sacred geometry for you. It's like the blueprint of everything that exists, from the tiniest atom to the vast galaxies above us. It's all about order, structure and harmony - the foundation of creation itself.

But wait, there's more. Sacred geometry is not just some abstract concept. It's a tool, my friend, a powerful one at that. By harnessing the energy of sacred geometric symbols and patterns, we can direct it towards bringing our desires to life. It's like having the universe on speed dial, ready to work its magic in manifesting our intentions.

Let's dive into some of these mind-blowing symbols, shall we? One of the big ones is the Flower of Life. Just picture this intricate web of circles, all overlapping and connecting in the most mesmerizing way. It's like staring into a cosmic kaleidoscope. This symbol is said to hold the keys to creativity and transformation. To make use of its power, all you gotta do is find or create a copy of it and display it prominently in your space. When you fix your gaze on this divine pattern, you're aligning yourself with the natural harmony of the universe, making it easier to bring your intentions to fruition.

Another heavy-hitter in sacred geometry is the Sri Yantra. It's this complex network of interlocking triangles, representing the Hindu goddess of abundance and manifestation. Talk about major girl power right there. You can meditate on this symbol or even create a physical representation like a crystal grid or a fancy piece of jewelry. When you connect with this sacred geometric energy, you're inviting abundance and manifestation to knock on your doorstep.

But hold up, we're not done yet. There's this mathematical miracle called the Fibonacci sequence. It's this never-ending pattern that crops up everywhere in nature, like the spirals of seashells and the growth of sunflowers. This sequence is the very embodiment of balance and order in the universe. By embracing this cosmic dance of numbers and incorporating it into our visualization and manifestation practices, we can align ourselves with the natural flow of energy and amplify our manifesting mojo.

Let me tell you a little secret. Combining sacred geometry with other manifestation techniques, like visualization and affirmations, is where the real magic happens. You can supercharge your visualization game by picturing your desired outcome within a sacred geometric shape. It's like you're painting your dreams onto this canvas of creation, infusing them with the power of the universe itself.

Oh, and affirmations? Yeah, they get a whole new level of power when you base them on sacred geometric patterns or symbols. It's like you're speaking the language of the cosmos, and the universe can't help but listen. By doing this, you amplify the effectiveness of your affirmations and align yourself with the very energies needed to make your desires come true.

In the end, my friend, sacred geometry is not just some esoteric concept. It's a tool that we can all use to enhance our manifestation practice. So, dive into this world of patterns and symbols and let the magic unfold. When you align yourself with the energy of sacred geometry, you open the doors to a whole new level of manifestation. Get ready for your intentions to manifest in ways you could never have imagined. It's time to embrace the power of sacred geometry and watch your dreams come to life.

Using Manifestation Rituals and Ceremonies

Using manifestation rituals and ceremonies has been a powerful tool in my personal journey towards achieving my desires and goals. These rituals and ceremonies hold significant meaning and effectiveness in the manifestation process. In this subchapter, I will provide step-by-step instructions on how to design personal rituals that can help you manifest your deepest desires.

The benefits of utilizing manifestation rituals and ceremonies are numerous. One of the positive aspects is that these rituals create a focused and intentional mindset. By incorporating specific actions and symbolism into our practices, we are able to align our thoughts and energy with our desires. This focused mindset allows us to manifest our desires more effectively.

Symbolism plays a crucial role in the manifestation process. When we choose symbols and objects that represent our intentions, we are able to enhance the power of our rituals. For example, using candles to represent illumination and clarity or crystals to amplify our intentions can greatly increase the potency of our manifestation practices. Symbols create a bridge between the physical and spiritual realms, allowing us to tap into the universal energy and manifest our desires more easily.

Ceremonies also play a significant role in the manifestation process. When we create a sacred space and invoke a sense of reverence through ceremonies, we are able to tap into the higher vibrations of the universe. This heightened state of consciousness allows us to align our energy with our desires, making the manifestation process more effective.

Rituals and ceremonies have the power to cultivate belief and confidence in the manifestation process. By consistently practicing these rituals, we build trust in ourselves and the universe. We begin to believe in our own ability to manifest our desires, and this belief becomes a powerful driving force in the manifestation journey.

Grounding our intentions and aligning our energy is another essential aspect of manifestation rituals. By incorporating grounding techniques and rituals into our practices, we are able to anchor our desires in the physical world. This alignment between our intentions and our energy creates a powerful magnetic force that attracts our desires towards us.

Designing personal rituals for manifestation requires careful consideration and intention. It starts with setting clear intentions and identifying specific desires. Clarity is key in the manifestation process, as it allows us to focus our energy and intentions towards a specific outcome.

Choosing appropriate symbols and objects to represent our intentions is another important aspect of designing personal rituals. These symbols act as anchors, reminding us of our desires and amplifying their manifestation. Visualization and affirmations also play a significant role in manifestation rituals. By visualizing our desires as already achieved and repeating affirmations that affirm our belief in the manifestation process, we are able to align our energy with our intentions.

Creating a ritual space and selecting appropriate timing is essential for the effectiveness of our rituals. This space should be free from distractions and interruptions, allowing us to fully immerse ourselves in the manifestation process. Elements such as candles, crystals, incense, and music can be incorporated into our rituals to enhance the energy and atmosphere.

Emotions and gratitude are powerful tools in amplifying the manifestation process. By infusing our rituals with positive emotions and expressing gratitude for the manifestation of our desires, we elevate our vibration and attract more abundance into our lives.

Concluding a ritual and releasing our intentions to the universe is a crucial step in the manifestation process. By letting go of attachment to outcomes and surrendering our desires to the universe, we create space for the manifestation to unfold in the most divine and perfect way.

While manifestation rituals and ceremonies are highly effective, there can be potential challenges or limitations to their efficacy. Consistency and commitment are key in practicing these rituals. It is important to maintain a regular practice and not give in to doubts or skepticism about their effectiveness.

Maintaining a positive mindset and avoiding attachment to outcomes is also crucial. It is important to trust in the universe and have faith that our desires will manifest in the perfect timing and way. Adapting and modifying rituals based on personal preferences and beliefs is also important, as each individual may resonate with different practices.

External factors such as distractions or interruptions can affect the effectiveness of our rituals. It is important to create a sacred and uninterrupted space for our practices. Patience and trust are also essential in the manifestation process. It takes time for our desires to manifest, and trusting in the process is key.

Enhancing the effectiveness of manifestation rituals and ceremonies can be achieved through additional tips and suggestions. Self-reflection and self-awareness play a significant role in the manifestation process. By examining our thoughts, beliefs, and actions, we are able to align them with our intentions and desires.

Gratitude and appreciation are also important in maintaining a high vibration. By expressing gratitude for what we already have and appreciating the manifestations that are already present in our lives, we attract more abundance into our reality. Self-care and self-love are essential in supporting manifestation rituals. Taking care of ourselves and nurturing our own well-being allows us to align with the energy of our desires more effectively.

Incorporating meditation and visualization techniques into our rituals can further enhance their effectiveness. These practices allow us to connect with our desires on a deeper level and amplify our manifesting power. Synchronicities and signs also play a role in the manifestation journey. Paying attention to these signs and following the guidance they provide can lead us towards the manifestation of our desires.

Aligning our actions with our intentions is crucial in manifesting our desired outcomes. Taking inspired action and moving towards our desires helps to solidify our commitment to the manifestation process. Lastly, faith and trust in the universe are essential. Believing in the power of manifestation and having unwavering faith that our desires will manifest is a key ingredient in the manifestation process.

In conclusion, utilizing manifestation rituals and ceremonies has been a transformative practice in my own life. By designing personal rituals and incorporating various elements into my practices, I have been able to manifest my desires with greater clarity and intention. The power of symbolism, ceremonies, and emotions have played a significant role in my manifestation journey. By addressing potential challenges and enhancing the effectiveness of our rituals, we can truly tap into the ultimate power of manifestation.

Harnessing the Power of Crystals and Gemstones

When it comes to manifestation, harnessing the power of crystals and gemstones is a game-changer. In this subchapter, we will dive into the energetic properties of these natural resources and explore how they can enhance our ability to manifest our desires. Crystals and gemstones have been used for centuries for their healing and protective qualities, but their role in the manifestation process is often overlooked. By understanding the importance and relevance of utilizing these powerful tools, we can unlock a whole new level of manifestation.

Understanding the Energetic Properties of Crystals and Gemstones:

To fully harness the power of crystals and gemstones, it's crucial to comprehend the concept of energetic properties. These precious stones possess unique energies that can influence and support our manifestation efforts. Each crystal and gemstone emit specific vibrations and frequencies that can align with our intentions and desires. Some stones, like amethyst, are known for their healing energies, while others, like citrine, are renowned for their manifestation energies. By exploring the different types of energies that crystals and gemstones can emit, we can tap into their full potential.

Selecting Crystals and Gemstones for Manifestation:

Choosing the right crystals and gemstones is essential for aligning them with our specific manifestations. Each stone has its own energetic properties, and by selecting ones that resonate with our desires, we can enhance our manifestation process. For example, if we seek abundance and prosperity, we might choose citrine or green aventurine, as they are known to attract wealth. On the other hand, if we are focusing on love and relationships, we may opt for rose quartz or emerald. By understanding the energetic properties of different crystals and gemstones, we can handpick the ones that will amplify our intentions.

Cleansing and Charging Crystals and Gemstones:

To maximize the energetic properties of crystals and gemstones, it is crucial to cleanse and charge them regularly. Over time, these stones can absorb negative energies and lose their effectiveness. Cleansing methods such as using water, sunlight, or other crystals can help restore their vibrancy. Charging techniques involve infusing them with intention and energy, ensuring that they are primed for manifestation. By incorporating cleansing and charging practices into our crystal routines, we can optimize the power of these natural resources.

Using Crystals and Gemstones in Manifestation Practices:

Incorporating crystals and gemstones into our manifestation practices can be a powerful tool for amplifying our intentions. There are various ways to utilize these stones, such as incorporating them into rituals, meditations, or daily practices. Placing crystals around our sacred space during meditation can help to create a high-vibrational environment conducive to manifestation. Carrying a crystal in our pocket or wearing it as jewelry can serve as a constant reminder of our intentions throughout the day. By integrating crystals and gemstones into our manifestation practices, we can create a powerful synergy between our thoughts, intentions, and the natural energies of these stones.

Combining Crystals and Gemstones for Amplified Manifestation:

While individual crystals and gemstones hold immense power, combining them can create a synergistic effect that amplifies our manifestation efforts. Certain stones complement each other, enhancing their energetic properties and magnifying the desired outcome. For example, combining amethyst and clear quartz can create a powerful connection between spiritual awareness and manifestation abilities. By exploring the combinations that resonate with our intentions, we can unlock a greater level of manifestation.

Programming Crystals and Gemstones for Specific Intentions:

Programming crystals and gemstones with specific intentions is a crucial step in utilizing their full potential. By setting clear intentions and infusing them into the energetic properties of these stones, we can direct their energies towards our desired manifestations. This can be done through visualization, meditation, or simply holding the stone and stating our intentions. By programming crystals and gemstones, we establish a powerful connection between our desires and the energies these stones possess.

Creating Crystal Grids for Manifestation:

Crystal grids are a powerful tool for enhancing the manifestation process. These grids involve arranging specific crystals and gemstones in a geometric pattern to amplify and direct their energies towards our intentions. By understanding the properties of different stones and their placement within the grid, we can create a powerful energy vortex that supports our manifestations. Whether it's for career growth, love, or spiritual awakening, crystal grids can serve as a potent tool in manifesting our desires.

Enhancing Manifestation with Crystal Elixirs and Jewelry:

Crystal elixirs and jewelry can be additional tools for aligning our energy with our desired manifestations. Crystal elixirs are made by infusing water with the energetic properties of specific stones, creating a potent drink that aligns our physical and energetic bodies. Wearing crystal jewelry, such as necklaces or bracelets, can serve as a constant reminder of our intentions and keep us connected to the energies of the stones throughout the day. By incorporating crystal elixirs and jewelry into our manifestation practices, we can further enhance our alignment with our desired outcomes.

Conclusion and Future Exploration:

In conclusion, harnessing the power of crystals and gemstones is a valuable tool in the manifestation process. By understanding the energetic properties of these natural resources, selecting the right stones, cleansing and charging them, and incorporating them into our practices, we can unlock their full potential. Additionally, exploring the power of combining stones, programming them with intentions, creating crystal grids, and utilizing crystal elixirs and jewelry can further amplify our manifestation efforts. This subchapter is just the beginning of our exploration into the power of crystals and gemstones. I encourage you to continue your research and personal experiences with these transformative tools to further enhance your manifestation abilities.

Incorporating Essential Oils and Aromatherapy

Manifestation is a concept that has gained significant attention in recent years, as individuals seek to harness their inner power and create their desired reality. Essential oils and aromatherapy are powerful tools that can enhance the manifestation process, helping individuals align their intentions and goals with the power of scent. In this chapter, we will explore the connection between manifestation and essential oils, as well as the benefits of incorporating aromatherapy into manifestation rituals.

Understanding the impact of scent on emotions:

Scent has a profound impact on our emotions, evoking specific responses that can either support or hinder our manifestation efforts. Different scents have the ability to elicit a range of emotions, from feelings of calm and relaxation to energy and motivation. By understanding this relationship between scent and emotions, we can strategically select essential oils that align with our desired emotional state and amplify the manifestation process.

The role of essential oils in supporting manifestation goals:

Essential oils play a crucial role in supporting manifestation goals by aligning with specific intentions and goals. Each essential oil carries its own unique properties and benefits that can be harnessed to enhance the manifestation process. For example, lavender essential oil is known for its calming properties, making it an ideal choice for individuals looking to manifest a state of inner peace and tranquility. On the other hand, citrus oils like lemon or orange can promote a sense of vitality and energy, supporting manifestation efforts related to productivity and motivation.

Selecting essential oils for manifestation:

When selecting essential oils for manifestation, it is important to consider individual preferences and associations with different scents. What may work for one person may not resonate with another. Therefore, it is essential to choose oils that personally resonate with you and align with your manifestation goals. By taking into account your unique preferences and associations with certain scents, you can create a powerful synergy between your intentions and the chosen essential oils.

Case study introduction:

In order to further illustrate the power of essential oils and aromatherapy in manifestation, we will now introduce a specific case study. This case study will provide a real-life example of how an individual incorporated essential oils into their manifestation practice and achieved their desired outcome. By examining their experiences and outcomes, we can gain valuable insights into the effectiveness of using essential oils for manifestation.

The individual's experience with essential oils and aromatherapy:

Let's dive into the personal experience of the individual in our case study. They embarked on a journey of incorporating essential oils and aromatherapy into their manifestation practice with a specific goal in mind. Throughout this process, they encountered various challenges, experienced moments of success, and gained profound insights into the power of scent and emotions in the manifestation process. By delving into their personal account, we can gain a deeper understanding of how essential oils and aromatherapy can transform our manifestation practice.

The impact of essential oils on the individual's emotions:

By closely examining the specific essential oils used in the case study, we can analyze their impact on the individual's emotional state. Essential oils have the ability to trigger emotional shifts, allowing individuals to align their emotions with their manifestation goals. Through this analysis, we can gain a deeper understanding of how these emotional shifts influenced the individual's ability to manifest their desired outcome.

Manifestation outcomes and the role of essential oils:

In this section, we will discuss the manifestation outcomes achieved by the individual in our case study. By examining the role that essential oils and aromatherapy played in their manifestation journey, we can gain insights into the effectiveness of these practices. Did the individual achieve their desired outcome? How did the use of essential oils contribute to their manifestation success? These questions will be explored in detail to highlight the powerful impact of essential oils on the manifestation process.

Lessons learned and recommendations:

Reflecting on the insights gained from the case study, we can draw valuable lessons and recommendations for using essential oils and aromatherapy in manifestation practices. What were the key takeaways from the individual's experience? How can others incorporate these practices into their own manifestation rituals? By sharing these lessons and recommendations, we hope to empower individuals to harness the ultimate power of manifestation through the use of essential oils and aromatherapy.

Conclusion and closing thoughts:

In conclusion, the use of essential oils and aromatherapy can greatly enhance the manifestation process. By understanding the connection between scent and emotions, selecting oils that align with specific intentions, and learning from real-life case studies, individuals can unlock their ultimate power of manifestation. The potential of essential oils and aromatherapy in creating our desired reality is immense, and by incorporating these practices into our manifestation rituals, we can truly transform our lives. So, why wait? Start harnessing the power of essential oils and embrace the journey of manifestation today.

Chapter 18: Overcoming Common Challenges in Manifestation

Dealing With Doubt and Skepticism

When it comes to the power of manifestation, doubt and skepticism can be major roadblocks on our journey towards achieving our desires. These negative thoughts and feelings can infiltrate our minds and hinder our ability to manifest our dreams into reality. It is essential, therefore, that we address and overcome doubt and skepticism in order to unlock the ultimate power of manifestation.

Doubt and skepticism can be defined as the lack of belief or trust in our own abilities or in the manifestation process itself. They often arise as a result of past failures or disappointments, societal conditioning, or a general sense of uncertainty. These doubts and skeptical thoughts can have a detrimental impact on our self-belief and trust in the manifestation journey.

Recognizing and acknowledging doubt and skepticism is the first step towards overcoming them. It is important to cultivate self-awareness and actively identify any doubts or skeptical thoughts that arise within us. By acknowledging these doubts and skepticism, we can then begin to address them and take steps towards overcoming them.

Building self-belief is crucial in order to overcome doubt and skepticism. Strategies such as positive affirmations and visualization techniques can help us reinforce our belief in our own abilities and in the power of manifestation. It is also important to set realistic goals and celebrate small manifestations along the way, as this will boost our self-confidence and reinforce our belief in the manifestation process. Additionally, practicing self-compassion and self-care is essential for building self-belief, as it allows us to nurture ourselves and cultivate a positive mindset.

Cultivating trust in the manifestation journey is another key aspect of overcoming doubt and skepticism. Techniques such as gratitude and mindfulness can help us build trust in the process by shifting our focus to the present moment and appreciating what we already have. Surrendering and letting go of attachment to outcomes is also crucial, as it allows us to trust that the universe or a higher power has our best interests at heart. By trusting in the process and relinquishing control, we open ourselves up to the infinite possibilities that lie ahead.

Overcoming doubt and skepticism through evidence is a powerful method of solidifying our belief in the manifestation process. Keeping a manifestation journal and documenting successful manifestations allows us to reflect on our achievements and remind ourselves of our manifesting abilities. Visualization exercises and manifestation techniques also play a significant role in building evidence and reinforcing our belief. Furthermore, seeking out testimonials and success stories from others who have successfully manifested their desires can provide us with inspiration and help us overcome any lingering doubts or skepticism.

Seeking support and guidance is vital in dealing with doubt and skepticism. Having mentors, coaches, or joining support groups can provide us with the encouragement and accountability we need to stay on track and overcome any challenges that arise. Sharing our experiences and challenges with like-minded individuals can also provide us with a sense of community and reassurance that we are not alone in our manifestation journey.

In order to gain a comprehensive understanding of doubt and skepticism in manifestation, it is important to explore cross-cultural perspectives. Different cultures approach doubt and skepticism in unique ways, and by learning from these perspectives, we can gain valuable insights and strategies. Each culture may have its own methods for building self-belief and cultivating trust in the manifestation journey, and adopting and adapting these strategies can be highly beneficial in overcoming doubt and skepticism.

In conclusion, doubt and skepticism can be major obstacles on our manifestation journey, but with the right techniques and mindset, we can overcome them. By recognizing and acknowledging doubt and skepticism, building self-belief, cultivating trust, seeking evidence, and seeking support and guidance, we can unlock the ultimate power of manifestation. Additionally, learning from cross-cultural perspectives can provide us with valuable insights and strategies to further enhance our manifestation journey. It is through addressing and overcoming doubt and skepticism that we can truly tap into our manifesting potential and create the life we desire.

Managing Impatience and Frustration

In this chapter, I want to dive into the topic of managing impatience and frustration, as it is a crucial aspect of the manifestation process. When we set our sights on a desired outcome, it is only natural to feel eager for it to materialize. However, when things don't happen as quickly as we hope, impatience and frustration can easily creep in, causing us to doubt and lose faith in the process.

Understanding Impatience and Frustration

Before we can effectively manage these emotions, it's important to first understand what they are and how they can affect our mental well-being and the overall manifestation process. Impatience is a feeling of restlessness or irritation when things don't happen on our desired timeline, while frustration stems from the inability to achieve a desired outcome. Both of these emotions can be detrimental to our manifestation journey, as they create a negative mindset and hinder our ability to attract what we desire.

Exploring the Manifestation Process

To better grasp the importance of managing impatience and frustration, let's take a closer look at the manifestation process itself. Manifestation often involves a waiting period, where the universe aligns the necessary circumstances to bring our desires into reality. This waiting period can be challenging, as it tests our patience and faith. However, it is crucial to understand that patience plays a vital role in allowing manifestations to unfold naturally. By maintaining a positive mindset and trusting in the process, we are more likely to attract our desired outcome.

Recognizing Triggers and Negative Thought Patterns

Impatience and frustration are often triggered by certain situations or thought patterns. By recognizing these triggers, we can begin to reframe our mindset and navigate through these emotions more effectively. It's important to identify common triggers, such as comparing our progress to others or dwelling on past failures. Additionally, negative thought patterns, such as self-doubt or fear of failure, can further exacerbate impatience and frustration. By becoming aware of these triggers and thought patterns, we can consciously choose to shift our focus and cultivate a more positive mindset.

Practicing Self-Awareness and Mindfulness

Self-awareness is a powerful tool in managing impatience and frustration. By cultivating present moment awareness through mindfulness techniques, we can better observe our thoughts and emotions without getting swept away by them. Mindfulness allows us to create space between our thoughts and our reactions, enabling us to respond with clarity and calmness. By integrating mindfulness practices into our daily routines, such as meditation or conscious breathing, we can maintain a positive mindset even during the waiting period.

Cultivating Patience

Developing patience is a skill that requires practice and conscious effort. It involves shifting our focus from the future to the present, embracing the journey rather than fixating solely on the desired outcome. Gratitude is a powerful tool in cultivating patience, as it allows us to appreciate the progress we have made so far and the lessons we are learning along the way. Setting realistic expectations is also crucial, as it prevents us from becoming overwhelmed by unrealistic timelines. By embracing the process and having faith in divine timing, we can nurture our patience and trust that the desired manifestation will unfold when the time is right.

Finding Support and Connection

During the waiting period, seeking support from like-minded individuals can be immensely beneficial. Connecting with others who are also on their manifestation journey can provide encouragement, guidance, and a sense of community. Online communities, support groups, or forums dedicated to manifestation practices can be great resources for finding support and connecting with individuals who share similar experiences. By sharing our own experiences and advice, we not only receive support but also contribute to the growth of others.

Creating a Positive Environment

Creating a positive and supportive environment is essential for maintaining a high vibrational energy during the waiting period. Surrounding ourselves with uplifting people and engaging in activities that bring us joy can significantly impact our mindset. By minimizing exposure to negativity, whether it be through news, social media, or toxic relationships, we can protect our energy and stay aligned with our desires. By consciously curating a positive environment, we create the ideal conditions for our manifestations to thrive.

Practicing Self-Care

Self-care is crucial during the manifestation process, especially when impatience and frustration arise. Engaging in activities that promote emotional well-being, such as exercise, meditation, or self-reflection, can help alleviate stress and maintain a positive mindset. Practicing self-compassion and self-forgiveness is equally important, as it allows us to be gentle with ourselves during moments of impatience or perceived setbacks. By prioritizing self-care, we create a solid foundation for our manifestation journey.

Maintaining Faith and Trust

Finally, maintaining faith and trust in the manifestation process is key. It's important to remember that delays or setbacks are often part of the journey and do not mean that our desires will not manifest. By continuously believing in our desired outcome, even when faced with challenges, we align ourselves with the universe's energy and allow it to work its magic. Surrendering to the process and trusting that everything is unfolding as it should cultivates a sense of peace and certainty that our desires will manifest in due time.

In conclusion, managing impatience and frustration is vital in the manifestation process. By understanding these emotions, recognizing triggers and negative thought patterns, practicing self-awareness and mindfulness, cultivating patience, finding support, creating a positive environment, practicing self-care, and maintaining faith and trust, we can navigate through the waiting period with grace and maintain a positive mindset. Remember, patience is a virtue, and by embracing the journey, we open ourselves up to limitless possibilities.

Navigating Setbacks and Obstacles

Navigating setbacks and obstacles is an essential aspect of the manifestation journey. It is important to understand the significance of these challenges and how they can either hinder or propel our progress towards our desires. In this subchapter, we will explore the common challenges and obstacles that individuals may encounter during their manifestation process. By reframing these challenges and finding opportunities for growth and learning, we can overcome them and continue on our path towards manifestation success.

Defining Terms:

Before delving deeper into the topic, let's establish a common understanding of key terms related to setbacks, obstacles, manifestation journey, reframing, and growth. Setbacks refer to any unexpected events or situations that hinder our progress. Obstacles, on the other hand, are specific challenges that we must overcome to achieve our desired outcomes. The manifestation journey encompasses the process of intentionally creating our reality through thoughts, beliefs, and actions. Reframing involves changing our perspective and finding positive meaning in challenging situations. Lastly, growth refers to personal development and expansion that occurs through overcoming obstacles and learning from setbacks. These terms are crucial in understanding the subchapter's objectives and will guide our exploration of navigating setbacks and obstacles on the manifestation journey.

Objectives and Scope:

The primary goal of this subchapter is to provide guidance on effectively navigating setbacks and obstacles encountered during the manifestation journey. To achieve this, we will cover a range of topics including identifying and overcoming setbacks, reframing challenges, and finding opportunities for growth and learning. By addressing these key areas, readers will gain practical strategies and insights to overcome obstacles and continue their progress towards manifestation success.

Methodology and Approach:

In this subchapter, we adopt a comprehensive approach that combines research, personal experiences, and expert insights. By drawing from a diverse range of sources, we aim to provide readers with a well-rounded understanding of navigating setbacks and obstacles. The content is organized and structured in a way that offers practical guidance and strategies to readers. Through a step-by-step approach, we aim to empower individuals to overcome challenges and manifest their desires with confidence.

Identifying Setbacks and Obstacles:

To effectively navigate setbacks and obstacles, it is crucial to first identify and acknowledge their presence. In this section, we will explore the different types of setbacks and obstacles that individuals may encounter on their manifestation journey. By recognizing and acknowledging these challenges, we can better prepare ourselves to overcome them and continue on our path towards manifestation success.

Overcoming Setbacks and Obstacles:

Once we have identified the setbacks and obstacles, the next step is to develop strategies and techniques for overcoming them. This section will introduce various approaches such as developing resilience, seeking support, and problem-solving. By applying these strategies in the context of the manifestation journey, readers can overcome obstacles and maintain their momentum towards their desired outcomes.

Reframing Challenges:

Reframing challenges is a powerful mindset shift that allows us to find opportunities for growth and learning in the face of setbacks and obstacles. This section will explain the concept of reframing and its importance in navigating challenges. We will discuss different techniques, including cognitive restructuring, perspective shifting, and gratitude practice, to help readers reframe challenges and find positive meaning in difficult situations.

Finding Opportunities for Growth and Learning:

Setbacks and obstacles can provide unique opportunities for personal growth and learning. In this section, we will explore how these challenges can serve as catalysts for transformation and expansion. By adopting a mindset that embraces these opportunities, readers can turn setbacks into valuable experiences that contribute to their manifestation journey.

Practical Tips and Takeaways:

To ensure that readers have actionable guidance to navigate setbacks and obstacles on their manifestation journey, we will compile practical tips and takeaways. These tips will summarize the key strategies and techniques discussed throughout the subchapter, providing readers with tangible steps to implement in their own lives.

In conclusion, navigating setbacks and obstacles is an essential aspect of the manifestation journey. By reframing challenges and finding opportunities for growth and learning, we can overcome these challenges and continue on our path towards manifestation success. Through a comprehensive approach, incorporating research, personal experiences, and expert insights, this subchapter aims to provide readers with the necessary tools to navigate setbacks and obstacles with confidence and resilience.

Maintaining a Positive Mindset During Challenging Times

Maintaining a positive mindset during challenging times is crucial for our overall well-being. In this subchapter, I will delve into the significance of cultivating positivity and shifting our perspective, as well as the detrimental effects of a negative mindset.

When we face adversity, it is natural to feel overwhelmed and discouraged. However, dwelling on negativity only exacerbates the situation, leading to increased stress, anxiety, and feelings of hopelessness. A negative mindset becomes a vicious cycle that traps us in a state of despair, hindering our ability to find solutions and move forward.

Shifting our perspective is the key to breaking free from this cycle. By consciously choosing to view challenges as opportunities for growth and positivity, we unlock the power of manifestation. It is in these difficult moments that we have the chance to tap into our inner strength and resilience, enabling us to overcome obstacles and achieve our goals.

Techniques for Cultivating a Positive Mindset

In order to cultivate a positive mindset, we must employ specific techniques that foster resilience, gratitude, the ability to find silver linings, and the practice of mindfulness and positive affirmations.

The first technique is cultivating resilience. Resilience is the ability to bounce back from adversity, and it is a skill that can be developed through various strategies. Practicing self-care is essential, as it allows us to recharge and maintain our physical and mental well-being. Seeking support from others is another crucial aspect of resilience, as it provides us with a network of individuals who can offer guidance, encouragement, and perspective. Furthermore, reframing challenges as opportunities for personal growth allows us to shift our mindset and approach difficulties with a sense of determination and optimism.

Finding gratitude is the second technique for cultivating a positive mindset. By consciously acknowledging and appreciating the positive aspects of our lives, we shift our focus from negativity to abundance. Practicing gratitude can be as simple as keeping a gratitude journal, where we write down three things, we are grateful for each day. This simple practice rewires our brain to focus on the positive, leading to a more optimistic outlook.

The third technique involves seeking silver linings. When faced with difficult situations, we can choose to find the silver linings – the hidden opportunities or positive aspects that may be present. This mindset shift allows us to reframe our challenges and see them as stepping stones towards growth and self-improvement. By focusing on the silver linings, we maintain a positive mindset even in the face of adversity.

Lastly, mindfulness and positive affirmations are powerful tools for maintaining a positive mindset. Mindfulness involves being fully present in the moment and observing our thoughts and emotions without judgment. This practice allows us to detach from negative thoughts and cultivate a sense of calm and clarity. Additionally, positive affirmations are statements that reinforce positive beliefs and encourage self-belief. By repeating affirmations such as "I am capable," "I am deserving," and "I am resilient," we reprogram our subconscious mind to align with our desired positive mindset.

Applying a Positive Mindset in Challenging Times

Real-life examples and case studies demonstrate the power of maintaining a positive mindset during challenging times. These stories illustrate how individuals have not only overcome adversity, but also experienced positive outcomes as a result. By studying these examples, we can gain inspiration and insights into how we can apply these principles in our own lives.

Incorporating positive mindset practices into our daily lives is crucial for lasting change. Practical suggestions include creating a gratitude journal, where we take a few moments each day to write down what we are grateful for. This practice shifts our focus to the positive aspects of our lives and sets the tone for a positive mindset. Additionally, practicing mindfulness through meditation or other mindfulness techniques helps us stay grounded and present, allowing us to respond to challenges with clarity and composure. Engaging in activities that bring us joy and fulfillment also plays a crucial role in maintaining a positive mindset, as it reminds us of the abundance of positivity that exists in our lives.

In conclusion, maintaining a positive mindset during challenging times is paramount for our well-being and success. By cultivating resilience, finding gratitude, seeking silver linings, and practicing mindfulness and positive affirmations, we can harness the power of manifestation and overcome obstacles with grace and determination. Let us embrace these techniques and integrate them into our daily routines, as they hold the key to unlocking our ultimate power of manifestation.

Chapter 19: The Law of Giving and Receiving

The Joy of Giving

As I set out on this journey of manifestation, I quickly realized that it's not just about receiving. The true essence of this power lies in giving as well. It's through acts of kindness and selflessness that we tap into a deeper level of fulfillment and joy. In this chapter, I invite you to explore with me the profound impact that giving to others can have on our lives and the various ways in which we can express our generosity.

Let's start with the sheer joy and fulfillment that comes from giving. When we offer our time, resources, or expertise to others, there's a sense of satisfaction that can't be matched. It's that warm feeling deep inside, knowing that we've made a positive impact in someone else's life. These moments of selflessness open our eyes to the interconnectedness of humanity and the power we have to uplift one another.

Did you know that giving actually activates the pleasure center of our brains? It releases endorphins, those feel-good hormones that create a sense of well-being. So, not only are we making others happy, but we're also boosting our own mental health. That's like a double dose of happiness!

Now let's explore the different ways we can give. There are countless ways to spread kindness and make a difference in the lives of those around us. Simple acts of kindness can have a profound impact on someone's day. A small gesture like holding the door open for a stranger or offering a helping hand to a friend can remind us of our shared humanity and the power of empathy. It's these little things that can create ripples of positivity in our communities and inspire others to pay it forward.

Another way to give is through charitable donations. By supporting organizations and causes that align with our values, we can make a direct impact on those in need. Whether it's donating money, clothing, or food, our contributions go a long way in providing comfort and support. It's a chance to share our blessings with those who are less fortunate.

But giving isn't just about material things. Our time and expertise are invaluable gifts that we can share with others. Volunteering at local organizations, mentoring individuals in our community, or simply offering our skills and knowledge can have a profound impact. By giving our time and expertise, we empower others to learn and grow, and we create meaningful connections that enrich our lives.

But here's the thing, the impact of giving doesn't stop with the immediate recipient. No, it has a ripple effect that can touch the lives of countless individuals. When we show kindness and compassion, we create a positive energy that inspires others to do the same. It's like a domino effect of goodness, spreading kindness and love throughout the world.

Research has actually shown that even observers of acts of kindness experience an uplift in their own moods. It motivates them to engage in kind acts themselves, creating a positive feedback loop. So, by giving, we not only make a difference in someone's life, but we also inspire others to make a difference too. It's like a chain reaction of kindness and compassion.

To truly experience the joy of giving, we must cultivate a mindset of abundance and gratitude. It's about recognizing the blessings in our own lives and expressing gratitude for them. When we practice daily gratitude exercises, we're reminded of what we have and it instills a sense of appreciation within us. And that naturally translates into a desire to share our blessings with others.

But let's not forget, giving should come from a place of authenticity and intention. It's important that it comes from a genuine place of care and compassion, rather than a sense of obligation or expectation. When we give without attachment to the outcome, we allow ourselves to experience the true joy that comes from helping others. It's about letting go and embracing the feeling of giving without expecting anything in return.

And finally, while individual acts of giving are significant, we shouldn't underestimate the power of collective giving. When like-minded individuals come together to support a common cause, the impact can be monumental. By joining forces with others who share our values and passions, we can amplify our impact and make a difference on a larger scale. Collective giving has the potential to create lasting change and address systemic issues that affect our communities.

In conclusion, the joy of giving is a profound experience that awakens our spirits and brings us closer to our true selves. It's not just about manifestation for ourselves, but also for others. By embracing acts of kindness, charitable donations, and sharing our time and expertise, we unlock the power of manifestation in the lives of others as well. Giving is an act of selflessness that connects us to the wider human family, reminding us of the potential we have to make a difference in the world. So, as we continue on our manifestation journey, let's remember the joy that comes from giving and embrace it fully. Together, through our generosity, we have the power to create a more compassionate and abundant world for all.

Receiving With Gratitude

Hey there! Welcome to this incredible chapter all about receiving with gratitude. We're about to embark on a journey that will show you just how important it is to be open to receiving and how it can bring abundance into your life. Get ready to dive deep, overcome blocks, and embrace the abundance that's waiting to burst into your world. Are you pumped? Because I am!

Picture this -- a luscious garden brimming with vibrant flowers. Now think about what would happen if those flowers stubbornly refused to open up their petals and soak in the sunlight and rain. Yeah, not so pretty anymore, right? Well, the same goes for us. We need to learn how to open ourselves up and receive the incredible abundance that life has to offer. By being receptive, we create the perfect space for blessings to pour into our lives.

But here's the thing: receiving can be a real challenge for some of us. We've been conditioned by society or perhaps we've had past experiences that shape our beliefs about receiving. It's time to shift that perspective, my friend. Receiving is not a sign of weakness or dependency, oh no. It's an empowering act that allows us to fully participate in the beautiful energy exchange of the universe. We're not just passive observers, we're active participants in this grand dance of giving and receiving.

You know what they say -- what goes around, comes around. Giving and receiving are like two peas in a pod; they're part of the same cycle. When we give with an open heart, we create a wondrous flow of energy that ensures we are supported and nourished in return. By embracing the act of receiving, we're acknowledging the interconnectedness of everything and keeping that cycle of abundance going strong.

Before we can let abundance in, we need to identify any blocks or limiting beliefs that might be standing in the way. It's time to do some soul-searching, my friend. These blocks can creep in when we feel unworthy, fear dependency, or carry guilt about receiving more than we give. But fear not! Through self-reflection and self-awareness, we can tear down those barriers and make space for abundance to enter our lives.

Here's a powerful technique to release those limiting beliefs: affirmations. Yep, positive statements are the real deal. By repeating affirmations like "I am worthy of receiving abundance" or "I gratefully receive all the blessings that come my way," we're rewiring our subconscious mind and aligning it with our desires. It's like reprogramming the software of your brain.

But wait, there's more! Inner child healing is another badass tool that can help you overcome those blocks. Our childhood experiences often shape our beliefs around receiving. So, let's reconnect with our inner child and heal any wounds or traumas that might be holding us back. By doing this, we're building a solid foundation for receiving with pure joy and gratitude.

Now, let's talk gratitude. This stuff is like a key that can unlock the doors of abundance. Seriously, it's magical. When we focus on all the blessings we already have in our lives, we create a positive mindset that attracts even more abundance. So, start a daily gratitude practice. Grab a pen and paper, and write down three things you're grateful for each day. Just watch as your abundance multiplies before your very eyes.

To truly embrace abundance, we need to trust the universe. Trust that it's got an infinite supply of blessings just waiting for us, and that everything we need will come to us at the perfect time. Trust allows us to let go of control and surrender to the beautiful flow of abundance. It's like surfing a wave of abundance, dude. Just ride it.

Last but not least, we need to nurture our self-worth. Embracing abundance starts with recognizing our own inherent worthiness. We are deserving of all the goodness that life has to offer, my friend. So, practice some self-love, self-care, and set healthy boundaries. Doing this reinforces our self-worth and creates a magnetic energy that attracts abundance effortlessly.

As we wrap up this mind-blowing chapter, take a moment to reflect on the awesomeness of embracing the act of receiving. By shifting our perspective, overcoming blocks, and allowing abundance to flow, we become magnets for blessings beyond our wildest dreams. So, open your heart, trust the process, and let gratitude guide you as abundance floods into your life. Remember, the universe is ready and waiting to shower you with blessings, my friend. All you gotta do is receive.

The Cycle of Giving and Receiving

You know, when I think about giving, I don't just think about handing over material possessions to someone in need. It goes so much deeper than that. Giving is like this powerful force that sets off a chain reaction in the universe. It's not just about what we physically give, but also the energy and intentions behind our actions.

I mean, think about it. When we give without expecting anything in return, we're creating this positive energy that just keeps flowing. It's like this never-ending cycle of abundance. What we put out into the world eventually finds its way back to us. It's that whole law of reciprocity thing.

And you know what's interesting? This whole giving and receiving thing play a huge role in manifestation. When we embrace a mindset of abundance and giving, we open ourselves up to this unlimited potential. We become like these channels that allow abundance to flow freely into our lives. It's like we're manifesting our desires effortlessly, just by being in alignment with the cycle of giving and receiving.

But here's the thing, it's not about giving just so we can get something in return. It's about giving from a place of genuine love and compassion. It's about giving without any expectations or attachments to specific outcomes. That's when the magic happens. When we give with pure intentions, when we create this space for miracles to occur.

You see, this whole cycle of giving and receiving is all about energy. Every action we take has this energetic frequency that bounces around the universe. So, when we give with love and kindness, we're emitting this high vibration that attracts similar frequencies back into our lives. It's like acts of kindness and generosity are magnets for unexpected blessings and opportunities.

To really be in alignment with this cycle, we have to cultivate a mindset of abundance. We have to let go of that scarcity, lack, and fear-based thinking. We have to believe that there's more than enough to go around, and that we're deserving of all the amazing things the universe has to offer. It's all about shifting our mindset and opening ourselves up to receiving the gifts that are meant for us.

Practicing gratitude is another awesome way to align ourselves with this cycle. By being grateful for what we already have, we're acknowledging the abundance that's already present in our lives. It's like we're sending out this signal of appreciation, and it attracts even more blessings and abundance. When we focus on what we're grateful for, we're actively participating in this cycle of give and take.

So, here's the thing about manifestation. Giving and receiving are not separate. They're like two sides of the same coin, equally important in creating a life of abundance. When we give, we create space for receiving. And when we receive, we create space for giving. It's this beautiful interconnectedness that keeps the flow of abundance going in our lives.

When we're in alignment with this cycle, our manifestations become even more powerful. By giving freely and abundantly, we're telling the universe that we're open and ready to receive. It's like this amazing energetic exchange that opens doors, removes obstacles, and makes our desires manifest effortlessly. We become co-creators with the universe, just dancing in harmony with this cycle of giving and receiving.

So, my friend, I really encourage you to embrace this cycle in your own manifestation journey. Give freely, show love to everyone, and create this space for miracles to happen. Trust in the incredible potential of the universe and your own ability to manifest your desires. As you align yourself with this cycle of giving and receiving, you'll see just how powerful it is in transforming your life. It's this undeniable truth that will guide you on your journey to manifestation.

Chapter 20: Conclusion

Reflecting on Your Transformation

In this subchapter, I invite you to reflect on your personal transformation throughout this book. Self-reflection is a powerful tool that allows us to acknowledge our growth and celebrate our progress. It provides us with an opportunity to delve deep within ourselves, gain clarity about our transformation journey, and appreciate the changes we have experienced.

One effective way to engage in self-reflection is through journaling. Journaling serves as a tangible record of our thoughts, emotions, and experiences throughout the transformation process. It allows us to track our progress, identify patterns, and gain valuable insights into our own growth. By putting our thoughts onto paper, we are able to examine them objectively and gain a fresh perspective.

Now, you might be wondering what exactly you should reflect on. That's where prompts for self-reflection come in. I have compiled a list of thought-provoking prompts for you to explore your thoughts, feelings, and behaviors throughout this book. These prompts will encourage you to dig deep within yourself and uncover hidden aspects of your transformation journey. They will help you gain a deeper understanding of yourself and your growth.

Acknowledging and celebrating our growth is an essential part of the transformation process. By recognizing and appreciating the changes we have experienced, we reinforce our commitment to personal growth. It is through this acknowledgment that we can truly embrace our transformation and continue on our journey with renewed enthusiasm.

But it doesn't stop there. Celebrating milestones and achievements is equally important. By celebrating our progress, we create a positive feedback loop that motivates us to keep going. Whether it's treating yourself to something special or sharing your achievements with loved ones, find ways to celebrate your progress and keep the momentum going.

Now, let's shift our focus to cross-cultural perspectives on transformation. Different cultures approach personal growth and self-reflection in unique ways. By exploring these perspectives, we can gain new insights and inspiration for our own transformation journey.

Culture A, for example, places a strong emphasis on community and interconnectedness. Their approach to personal transformation is rooted in collective growth. By examining the practices, beliefs, and values of Culture A, we can gain a deeper understanding of the importance of community support in our own transformation.

Culture B, on the other hand, places a greater emphasis on individuality and self-expression. Their approach to personal growth and self-reflection involves introspection and self-discovery. By exploring Culture B's practices and beliefs, we can gain insights into the power of individuality in our transformation journey.

By comparing these cross-cultural perspectives, we can identify key insights and patterns that emerge. These insights can then inform our own personal transformation journey. Take the time to reflect on these comparative insights and consider how they align with your own values and goals. Use them as a guide to further enhance your transformation process.

In conclusion, reflecting on your transformation is a crucial step in your personal growth journey. By journaling, engaging in self-reflection, acknowledging your growth, and celebrating your progress, you can continue to evolve and transform. Additionally, by exploring cross-cultural perspectives on transformation, you can gain new insights and inspiration for your own journey. Embrace the power of self-reflection and let it guide you towards ultimate manifestation.

Embracing a Lifelong Journey of Manifestation

I've always believed that manifestation is a lifelong journey, and it's a belief I want to share with you in this subchapter. Understanding that manifestation is not a one-time event, but a continuous process is crucial for unlocking its true power. In this book, I'll be sharing techniques and principles that can guide you on this lifelong journey of manifestation.

Manifestation is not something that happens overnight or through a single act. It's an ongoing practice that requires consistent effort and dedication. Viewing it as a lifelong journey allows us to embrace the process, rather than focusing solely on the end result. By approaching manifestation with this mindset, we can experience a range of benefits, such as increased clarity, personal growth, and a deeper connection with our desires.

Consistent practice is key in the manifestation journey. It's not enough to sporadically apply manifestation techniques; we must make it a regular part of our lives. By consistently practicing manifestation, we can harness its power to create significant results. Take, for example, the story of Sarah, who diligently visualized her dream job every day for six months. Eventually, she landed the exact position she had envisioned. Consistency pays off.

Self-reflection is another crucial aspect of the manifestation process. By regularly reflecting on our thoughts, beliefs, and patterns, we can identify any limiting beliefs or self-sabotaging behaviors that may be hindering our manifestations. Self-reflection allows us to course-correct and grow as we continue on our journey of manifestation. It's through this ongoing self-reflection that we can experience true transformation and alignment with our desires.

Patience is a virtue that cannot be overlooked in the manifestation journey. It's easy to become discouraged or frustrated when our desires don't manifest immediately. However, patience allows for the gradual unfolding of our desires, ensuring that they are built on a solid foundation. Look at the story of Jack, who patiently worked towards his goal of financial abundance for several years. His patience paid off when he finally achieved long-lasting wealth. Patience is the key to enduring manifestations.

While the manifestation journey is undoubtedly transformative, it's not without its challenges and setbacks. It's important to acknowledge that setbacks are an inevitable part of the process. Instead of viewing them as failures, we can see them as opportunities for growth and learning. By staying committed to our manifestation practice and implementing strategies to overcome challenges, we can navigate through any obstacles that come our way.

Now, I understand that some readers may approach the idea of manifestation as a lifelong journey with skepticism or doubt. They may have misconceptions or objections about the effectiveness of ongoing manifestation practice. However, countless examples and evidence support the power of lifelong manifestation. Look at individuals like Oprah Winfrey, Tony Robbins, and Elon Musk, who have consistently manifested their dreams throughout their lives. Their success is a testament to the effectiveness of manifestation as a lifelong practice.

Furthermore, manifestation is not limited to short-term goals. It can be applied to long-term aspirations and desires as well. Whether it's a fulfilling career, a loving relationship, or a vibrant state of health, manifestation can help us manifest and sustain our long-term dreams. The key is to consistently apply manifestation techniques and stay committed to our desires over time.

While it's natural to feel burnt out or fatigued on the manifestation journey, there are strategies we can employ to maintain motivation and energy in the long term. It's essential to prioritize self-care and create balance in our lives. Taking breaks, practicing self-care rituals, and seeking support from loved ones can help us recharge and stay aligned with our manifestation goals.

Lastly, the lifelong nature of manifestation can sometimes feel overwhelming. Breaking the journey into smaller goals and milestones can alleviate this overwhelm. By setting achievable targets and celebrating each manifestation along the way, we can stay focused and motivated on our journey. Remember, manifestation is not a sprint; it's a marathon.

In conclusion, embracing a lifelong journey of manifestation is essential for unlocking its true power. By understanding that manifestation is a continuous process, practicing consistently, reflecting on our beliefs, practicing patience, overcoming challenges, and addressing common objections, we can harness the ultimate power of manifestation. So, let's embark on this lifelong journey together and manifest our wildest dreams.

The Limitless Potential of Your Thoughts and Intentions

When we take a moment to truly grasp the infinite power within our thoughts and intentions, we realize that we possess an extraordinary ability to shape our reality. It is a power that lies dormant within each and every one of us, waiting to be unleashed and harnessed. The importance of embracing this power cannot be overstated, for it holds the key to manifesting our deepest desires and achieving our wildest dreams.

The Power of Positive Thinking

Positive thinking is not just a cliché; it is a fundamental aspect of manifesting our dreams. Our thoughts and intentions have the ability to create a positive mindset, which in turn attracts abundance and success into our lives. By shifting our focus towards positivity and envisioning the realization of our dreams, we create a magnetic force that draws those dreams closer to us. It is through positive thinking that we tap into the limitless potential of the universe.

Visualizing and Believing

Visualization and belief are powerful tools that aid us in manifesting our desires. By vividly visualizing the outcomes we wish to achieve, we activate the creative power of our minds and set the wheels of manifestation in motion. Furthermore, strong beliefs play a pivotal role in the manifestation process. When we truly believe in our ability to manifest our dreams, we align ourselves with the energy of success and open ourselves up to the infinite possibilities that lie before us.

Overcoming Limiting Beliefs

Limiting beliefs can act as barriers to our manifestation efforts. These beliefs are often deeply ingrained within us, and they have the potential to hinder our progress. It is essential that we recognize and confront these limiting beliefs in order to move forward. By identifying the root causes of our self-imposed limitations and implementing strategies to overcome them, we can create a pathway towards manifesting our desires with greater ease and efficiency.

Taking Inspired Action

While thoughts and intentions are undeniably powerful, they must be accompanied by inspired action. It is through action that we bring our dreams closer to reality. By taking deliberate steps in alignment with our thoughts and intentions, we actively participate in the manifestation process. It is important to remember that manifestation is not solely a passive practice; it requires our active engagement and commitment.

Harnessing the Law of Attraction

The Law of Attraction is a universal principle that plays a significant role in the manifestation process. Simply put, like attracts like. By aligning our thoughts, intentions, and actions with the energy we wish to attract, we set in motion a chain of events that leads to the manifestation of our desires. To effectively harness the Law of Attraction, we must develop an understanding of its principles and utilize strategies that resonate with our individual goals and aspirations.

Cultivating Gratitude and Positivity

Gratitude and positivity are invaluable assets in the manifestation journey. When we cultivate a mindset of gratitude, we shift our focus towards abundance and open ourselves up to receiving more of what we desire. Practices such as gratitude journaling and affirmations help us to rewire our thought patterns and embrace a positive mindset. By consistently nourishing ourselves with gratitude and positivity, we create a fertile ground for our dreams to flourish.

Letting Go of Resistance and Attachment

Releasing resistance and attachment to outcomes is a crucial step in the manifestation process. Often, we hold onto rigid expectations and cling to specific outcomes, which can hinder the natural flow of manifestation. Surrendering control and trusting in the universe's wisdom allows us to let go of resistance and embrace the magic of the unfolding journey. It is through this surrender that we open ourselves up to the limitless possibilities that exist beyond our limited perceptions.

Aligning with Divine Timing

Divine timing is an integral part of the manifestation process. Trusting in the timing of the universe requires patience, faith, and a deep sense of knowing that everything is unfolding in perfect alignment with our highest good. By aligning ourselves with divine timing, we allow the universe to orchestrate the perfect sequence of events that will lead us towards the manifestation of our dreams. Countless stories and examples demonstrate the transformative power of aligning with divine timing and the remarkable results it can yield.

Living in Abundance and Empowerment

In conclusion, I encourage you, dear reader, to embrace a state of abundance and empowerment. Recognize your inherent ability to shape your reality and manifest your wildest dreams. Through the power of thoughts and intentions, positive thinking, visualization, and belief, overcoming limiting beliefs, taking inspired action, harnessing the Law of Attraction, cultivating gratitude and positivity, letting go of resistance and attachment, and aligning with divine timing, you have the power to manifest a life beyond your wildest imagination. Live in the knowing that the universe is conspiring in your favor, and allow yourself to bask in the joy and fulfillment that come from living a life of purpose and intention. The power to manifest is within you, waiting to be awakened.

BONUS Chapter: Manifesting a Sustainable Future

Conscious Consumption and Minimalism

Alright, folks, let's dive deeper into this whole manifestation journey we're on and talk about two things that are absolutely crucial: conscious consumption and minimalism. I know, I know, it sounds like some fancy mumbo jumbo, but trust me, it's way more than that. These practices not only benefit our own well-being but also have a massive impact on our lovely planet. So, hang on tight as we unravel the magic of conscious consumption and minimalism and how they can help us live a more sustainable lifestyle.

Now, let's start with conscious consumption. Picture this: a world drowning in an ocean of consumerism and materialism. It's pretty overwhelming, right? Well, it's time we wake up and shake things up. Conscious consumption is all about making deliberate and mindful choices when it comes to what we buy and use. It's about understanding the environmental and social impact of our choices and making choices that align with our values. Sounds fancy, I know, but it's actually pretty simple once we start questioning our motivations behind our desire for things and realizing the true value they bring to our lives. We can make more sustainable choices that make sense to us.

And speaking of minimalism, this bad boy goes hand in hand with conscious consumption. It's like the sidekick that makes our sustainability journey even more powerful. Minimalism is about prioritizing quality over quantity, about focusing on the things that truly bring us joy. By embracing minimalism, we declutter our lives, both physically and mentally, creating space for what really matters. It's like a breath of fresh air, freeing up our minds and allowing us to appreciate the little things that add true meaning to our lives.

Now let's get to the nitty-gritty of reducing our environmental impact. First things first, we gotta choose sustainable and ethical products. Yeah, I know it's not always easy to find them, but it's worth the effort. We can opt for items that are produced in a way that doesn't harm our lovely planet and that treat workers fairly. It's like casting our vote for a more sustainable future.

But wait, it doesn't end there. We can also find joy in second-hand and upcycled items. Yup, thrifting, swapping, and repurposing are not just cool trends, they're like little acts of creativity and resourcefulness. Not only do they cut down on waste, but they also contribute to the circular economy and keep stuff out of those monstrous landfills.

Oh, and let's not forget about the power of conscious consumer habits. It's all about those small actions that make a big difference. Using reusable bags, bottles, and containers instead of their single-use counterparts can seriously reduce our plastic waste. And hey, composting organic waste and recycling diligently are like high-fives to the environment. We're talking about conserving resources and showing Mother Earth some serious love.

Okay, folks, now let's jump into the world of minimalism. It all starts with decluttering our spaces and letting go of the stuff we really don't need. By clearing out the excess, we make room for clarity, peace, and intentionality. It's like hitting the reset button on our lives and creating a space that truly reflects who we are.

And oh boy, let's not forget about the capsule wardrobe. I don't know about you, but that concept speaks to my soul. It's all about curating a small collection of clothing items that can be mixed and matched, so we simplify the process of getting dressed. And not only that, but we also reduce our environmental impact by investing in high-quality pieces that align with our personal style and values. It's like saying goodbye to fast fashion and hello to a more intentional and sustainable approach to fashion.

But hey, minimalism doesn't just stop at our physical spaces. Nope, it extends to our digital lives too. We're talking about decluttering our digital world and setting some boundaries for our device usage. It's all about organizing and deleting unnecessary files, unsubscribing from email lists that clutter up our inbox, and taking control of our online presence. By simplifying our digital footprint, we reclaim our precious time and attention. It's like giving ourselves a digital detox and finding some peace in this chaotic online world.

So, my friends, let's wrap this all up. By integrating conscious consumption and minimalism into our lives, we're not only reducing our impact on the environment, but we're also nourishing a sustainable mindset. These practices remind us of the interconnectedness of all living beings and the significance of preserving our Earth for future generations. As we continue on our manifestation journey, let's embrace conscious consumption and minimalism as these powerful tools that can help us create a more harmonious and sustainable world.

Connecting With Nature

Hey there, my fellow nature lovers! Buckle up, because in this chapter, we're diving deep into the enchanting world of nature, uncovering its miraculous healing powers, and unraveling the significance of forging a stronger bond with Mother Nature. Brace yourselves, because through this journey, not only will we experience personal growth, but we'll also become fierce advocates for preserving our incredible planet.

Section 1: The Healing Power of Nature:

1.1 Discovering the Proven Benefits:

Let me tell you something mind-blowing, guys. Researchers have delved into this topic, and guess what? Immersing ourselves in nature has been scientifically proven to work wonders on our mind, body, and soul. It's like a magical elixir that washes away stress, anxiety, and even gives our immune system a much-needed boost. Nature really knows how to work its magic!

1.2 Nurturing the Mind, Body, and Spirit:

Close your eyes and picture this: the sweet melodies of birds chirping, vibrant flowers painting the landscape, and that earthy aroma that fills your lungs. When you're one with nature, all your senses ignite, and the present moment wraps you in a warm embrace. It's a holistic healing experience that rejuvenates your mind, body, and spirit in ways you can't even imagine.

1.3 Reconnecting with our True Nature:

In the hustle and bustle of our tech-infused lives, we often forget our roots, our intrinsic connection to the natural world. But fret not, my friends, for immersing ourselves in nature is like hitting the reset button. It taps into our primal instincts, reignites our bond with the Earth and every living creature on it. It's time to rediscover our true nature.

Section 2: Cultivating a Deeper Relationship with Nature:

2.1 Mindfulness in Nature:

Stay with me here because this is huge. Once we learn to be fully present in nature, we unlock a whole new level of awe and appreciation. Whether it's wandering through a tranquil forest or simply observing a flower bloom, practicing mindfulness in nature broadens our connection with the world around us. It's like wearing glasses that allow us to see the intricate beauty and abundance that otherwise goes unnoticed.

2.2 Sacred Rituals and Nature:

Guys, it's time to unleash our inner mystics. Incorporating sacred rituals centered around nature takes our connection even deeper. What do I mean? Picture this: gratitude ceremonies where we pour our hearts out, expressing love and thanks to the Earth. Or how about tree planting ceremonies, where every sapling becomes a symbol of our respect and commitment to our beloved planet.

2.3 Immersion in Natural Environments:

Let's talk about those jaw-dropping natural environments beyond our backyard, shall we? From national parks that make your heart skip a beat to lush forests and breathtaking beaches, these places are powerhouses of connection. Take a trip, my friends. Surround yourself with the awe-inspiring beauty of these spots, and feel yourself being woven into the tapestry of nature. It's there that we truly understand the fragile interconnection of every living being and the delicate balance of our world.

Section 3: Becoming an Advocate for Environmental Preservation:

3.1 Understanding the Importance of Preservation:

Hold up, folks. Are you feeling that burning passion deep within your souls? That's the fire of understanding, my friends. Our deep connection with nature imparts upon us a profound comprehension of its vulnerability and the ever-pressing need to protect it. We realize that by safeguarding the environment, we ensure a future for our beloved planet and every creature that calls it home.

3.2 Taking Action: Advocating for Change:

We're warriors now, locked and loaded with passion. Our connection with nature naturally propels us towards advocating for change. How do we do it? By spreading the word about sustainable practices, throwing our support behind conservation organizations, and hot damn, calling out environmental injustices. We're champions of the Earth, my friends.

3.3 Manifesting Positive Change:

Feel the power surging through your veins? By actively participating in preservation efforts, we bring about change not only within ourselves but in the entire world. With every action, every intention, we contribute to a collective consciousness that's laser-focused on Earth's well-being and future generations. We're making moves, people, and this is just the beginning.

Conclusion:

Well, amigos, we've embarked on a wild ride through the healing power of nature and the importance of connecting with it. By forging a deeper relationship with our planet, we unlock transformative personal growth, and we become fierce protectors of the environment. So, let's hold hands and march forward, for our actions and dedication have the power to manifest positive change in our world. Let our love for Mother Earth radiate through every single thing we do, as we dedicate ourselves to preserving this beautiful planet, we call home.

You know what? When it comes to being more sustainable, we can all make a difference with even just little changes in our daily routines. Like instead of using those flimsy plastic bags, why not rock some reusable shopping bags? And forget about those single-use plastic water bottles, grab yourself a refillable one. It's crazy how these small choices can really add up and make a big impact on the environment.

But it doesn't stop there. Saving energy is a biggie too. Just think about turning off the lights when you're not using them or unplugging those electronics that are just sitting there sucking up power. And let's not forget about those energy-efficient appliances - they're not only good for the earth, but they're also gonna save you some serious cash in the long run.

Now, here's where things get interesting. Supporting businesses that care about sustainability is the way to go. Look out for those companies that use organic, fair-trade, and cruelty-free materials. When we show these companies that we care about sustainability, we're sending a loud and clear message to other industries that it's time to step up their game.

And when it comes to getting from point A to point B, why not mix it up a little? Instead of driving everywhere, maybe consider hopping on public transportation, carpooling with friends, or even hoofing it or biking if you can. And don't forget about alternative fuel options like hybrid or electric cars. Or, for shorter distances, a bike or scooter might do the trick. It's all about reducing those carbon emissions, baby.

Now let's talk about food, my friend. It's all about supporting local farmers and organic produce. Hit up those farmers' markets or join a CSA program to get your hands on some good stuff. Not only are these initiatives promoting sustainable farming practices, but they're also cutting down on all those carbon emissions from shipping food long distances. Oh, and if you're up for it, try going plant-based or at least cut back on the meat a little. Animal agriculture has a huge carbon footprint, so every little bit helps.

Guys, water is precious. And we need to do our part to conserve it. Take shorter showers, fix any leaks you've got going on, and use rainwater to water your plants. And hey, there are some pretty cool water-saving technologies out there too, so why not look into those? And if you've got some graywater hanging around, like from washing dishes or your clothes, put it to good use for watering your plants. Waste not, my friend.

Alright, let's move on to fashion. Fast fashion is not cool. Like at all. It's horrible for the environment and completely takes advantage of people's labor. So instead of buying into that, think about buying less but investing in quality pieces. And look out for those brands that are all about sustainable and ethical practices. Oh, and don't forget to get creative with what you already have. Fix your clothes, repurpose them, whatever it takes to extend their life.

And last but not least, let's talk about waste management. Recycling and composting, my friends. They're game-changers. By sorting our waste properly and making sure recyclable materials actually get recycled, we're doing our part to create a more circular economy. And how about striving for zero waste? That means making smart choices about packaging, using reusable or refillable products, and adopting a more minimalist lifestyle. It's all about living with intention, my friends.

So, there you have it. Incorporating sustainable practices into our daily lives is not just a trendy thing to do, but it's also crucial for the well-being of our beautiful planet. Let's make reducing waste, conserving energy, supporting eco-friendly businesses, making conscious transportation and food choices, conserving water, choosing sustainable fashion, and managing our waste responsibly a non-negotiable part of our lives. Together, we have the power to create a future where our planet thrives.

Inspiring Others to Live Sustainably

As I set off on my transformative journey, a burning desire to inspire and empower others to embrace sustainable living took hold of me. I wanted to share my knowledge and passion, to be a catalyst for positive change for our beloved planet. In this chapter, I'll be your guide, showing you how to captivate and educate others about sustainable living, armed with effective strategies that will make you an unstoppable force of transformation.

4. Discovering Your Motivation:

Before you can even think about inspiring others, you've got to dig deep and uncover your own motivation for living sustainably. Take a moment to reflect on your personal journey and the impact it has had on your own life. Are you all about reducing waste? Or maybe conserving energy? Perhaps promoting biodiversity is your mantra? No matter what drives you, embrace it with your whole heart. Authenticity is the secret ingredient that will attract others to your cause like moths to a flame.

5. Educating Yourself:

To truly make a difference, you must equip yourself with a wealth of knowledge about sustainable living practices. Stay up to date with the latest research and developments in renewable energy, waste reduction, and ethical consumerism. Being a well-informed guru will give you the credibility you need to confidently answer questions and address concerns.

6. Tailoring Your Message:

Once you've mastered the art of sustainable living, it's time to customize your message to resonate with different audiences. Everyone has their own interests and priorities, so it's important to adapt accordingly. For instance, when talking to parents, emphasize the benefits of raising eco-conscious kids and the lasting impact it can have on their future. When dealing with business folk, highlight the economic advantages of embracing sustainable practices. By understanding your audience and customizing your message, you'll effortlessly capture their attention and ignite the flames of action within them.

7. Effective Communication Strategies:

Communication is the key to truly inspire and educate others about sustainable living. Here are some strategies to include in your arsenal:

- Use language that the everyday person can understand. Avoid technical jargon and make sustainability concepts relatable to their daily lives.

- Stories have incredible power. Share your own experiences and the challenges you've faced in adopting sustainable practices. By showing others that change is possible, you make sustainability more accessible.

- Be an active listener and engage in meaningful conversations. Respectfully listen to their concerns and perspectives. By understanding where they're coming from, you can address their doubts and provide relevant information.

- Provide practical tips and resources. Embarking on a sustainable journey can be overwhelming, but by offering tangible steps and information about local recycling programs, farmers' markets, and eco-friendly products, you make it easier for people to take those first small steps.

- Demonstrate the benefits. Show others how sustainable living can directly benefit them. For example, tout the cost savings of energy-efficient appliances or the health advantages of organic food. Paint a vivid picture of the positive outcomes to create an irresistible case for change.

- Collaborate and empower others. Encourage people to get involved by creating opportunities for collaboration. Organize community clean-up days, volunteer at local sustainability events, or even host workshops on sustainable living. By giving others, the power to be agents of change, you instill a sense of ownership and collective responsibility.

8. Leading by Example:

One of the most impactful ways to inspire others is by living your own life in alignment with your values. Let your actions speak for themselves. Be conscious of your consumption habits, prioritize renewable energy sources, and minimize waste. By embodying sustainable living, you become an undeniable testament to its possibilities and inspire those around you to follow suit.

9. Overcoming Resistance:

Change isn't always met with open arms. Some may resist the idea of embracing sustainable living. When faced with resistant individuals, approach them with compassion and understanding. Address their concerns and combat their misconceptions with evidence-based information. Remember, change takes time and patience. Plant the seeds of curiosity and allow them to bloom in due course.

10. Empowering a Sustainable Community:

As you continue to inspire and educate others, aim to create a sense of community among like-minded individuals. Foster networking, collaboration, and the exchange of ideas. By building a support system, your impact will be amplified, and you'll become part of a larger movement working towards a sustainable future.

In conclusion, inspiring and educating others about sustainable living is an honorable endeavor that demands passion, knowledge, and effective communication. By understanding your motivations, tailoring your message, and utilizing effective strategies, you can become a formidable agent of change. Remember to lead by example, collaborate with others, and empower your community. Together, we have the power to create a sustainable future for generations to come.

Manifestation Script
MAKE THE LAW OF ATTRACTION WORK FOR YOU

Are You Ready to Manifest?

What do you want to manifest into your life ?

____

____

____

____

What don't you like about your current situation? Why not?

____

____

____

____

How are your current thoughts and mindset affecting your ability to manifest your dream life?

____

____

____

____

Are you truly ready to change your energy and attract your dream life? How do you know?

____

____

____

____

Date ________________________ S M T W T F S

Today's Affirmation

____

TODAY I'M GRATEFUL FOR   TODAY I'M LOOKING FORWARD TO

I am manifesting...   ## Ideas and Daydreams

1. ________________________
2. ________________________
3. ________________________

WHAT I NEED TO DO TODAY

- ○ ______________________
- ○ ______________________
- ○ ______________________
- ○ ______________________
- ○ ______________________
- ○ ______________________
- ○ ______________________
- ○ ______________________
- ○ ______________________
- ○ ______________________

Today's Mood   SOMETHING GOOD THAT
                             HAPPENED TODAY
1 2 3 4 5 6 7 8 9 10

Negative   **Positive**

Envision Your Income

You head to the bank one morning to get some money out of the ATM. You take out the money, see your remaining balance and softly smile to yourself. You made it. You are finally where you want to be financially and feel at peace.

What do you do with the rest of your day? How are you making your money? How do you feel? Channel the energy you want to feel and journal about it below. Write in the present tense as if it has already come true!

YOUR MONTHLY INCOME

MY LIFE IS ....

____

____

____

____

____

____

____

____

____

____

Money Manifest Affirmations

Saying positive affirmations every day will help you overcome any negative thoughts and limiting beliefs you have surrounding money. The brain is very powerful because your thoughts become your reality! Write down your own money affirmations in the PRESENT tense as if you are already the person you want to be. "I am" statements are especially powerful!

Examples of Money Affirmations

- Money comes to me easily
- I am a money magnet
- I naturally attract good fortune
- I am creating constant wealth and abundance
- I deserve to be paid for my time, skills, and talents
- I am grateful for the wealth I have now and the wealth coming to me
- Every dollar I spend and give comes back to me
- I am able to check my bank account without anxiety
- I am a wealthy entrepreneur

Your Daily Affirmations

Say at least 3 of these affirmations every single day to train your brain!

1. I AM...
2. I AM...
3. I AM...
4. I AM...
5.
6.
7.
8.
9.
10.

Manifestation Clarity

What do you want to manifest?

Why do you want it?

What steps do you need to take to accomplish your goal?

How will you feel when you get it?

Manifestation Timeline

Write down your goals 1 month from now, 6 months from now and 1 year from now!

One Month

WHAT I WANT TO HAVE

HOW I WANT TO FEEL

Six Months

WHAT I WANT TO HAVE

HOW I WANT TO FEEL

One Year

WHAT I WANT TO HAVE

HOW I WANT TO FEEL

Letter to the Universe

Writing to the universe can help you manifest the money you want into your life if you approach it with positivity and gratitude. Start your letter off describing your current circumstance, discuss your problems or worries and then humbly ask the universe for what you want. Be specific and write about your desired outcome in the present tense. i.e. *I am having so much fun on my trip to Thailand.* End the letter by thanking the Universe and then let the letter go! Put it away, rip it up or burn it but do not obsess over it. Release your worries and attachment and simply wait for your manifestation to come true.

Dear Universe,

The 3-6-9 Method

The 3-6-9 Method is a powerful approach to manifest your desires through written affirmations. Aligning with principles inspired by Nikola Tesla and Abraham-Hicks, this technique involves writing a specific affirmation three times in the morning, six times in the afternoon, and nine times at night for 33 consecutive days.

Tesla, renowned for his innovative ideas, considered the numbers 3, 6, and 9 as divine and believed in their profound significance in nature and the universe. The method integrates the concept of focusing on an affirmation for 17 seconds, drawing from Abraham-Hicks teachings. This extended focus aims to align your energy with the desired outcome.

When crafting your manifestation, begin with expressions of gratitude, incorporate the emotions and benefits your desired outcome will bring, and conclude with the phrase "into my life." For instance, expressing gratitude for financial alignment and manifesting RS 5,00,000 into your bank account, brings security, excitement, and happiness.

Crucially, belief is paramount. You must not just desire the manifestation but genuinely believe it will occur. Focus on the emotions associated with your goal's achievement, envisioning how it will feel when it materializes.

Consistency is key. Regularly writing your manifestation reinforces the energy alignment needed for it to come true. Doubt and worry are counterproductive, as they can hinder the manifestation process. If doubts persist, consider starting with a more achievable goal, aligning your energy with a goal that feels realistic and attainable, such as manifesting RS 50,000.

Remember, the energy you emit must align with what you seek to attract. Stay committed to the process, maintain a positive mindset, and watch as your manifestations unfold

Writing your manifestation

When writing your manifestation, start with gratitude, add in the emotions/things your desired outcome will provide, and end it with "into my life"

i.e. I am so thankful to the universe for aligning my energy to attract Rs. 5,00,000 into my bank account and giving me financial security, excitement, and happiness in my life.

Things to Remember

- You can't just want your manifestation to come true, you have to believe it will come true and that it is only a matter of when.
- You should be focusing on how you will feel when your manifestation comes true.
- Imagine how you will feel when that Rs. 5,00,000 hits your account so you can align with that energy.
- Stay consistent with writing your manifestation for it to actually come true
- If you are constantly doubting or worrying that your manifestation will come true, it won't! You need to match your energy to what you seek to attract.
- If you are experiencing a lot of self-doubt, try starting over with a goal that is more realistic to you. For instance, manifest 50,000 instead of Rs. 5,00,000

3-6-9 Manifestation

Write the same manifestation 3 times in the morning, 6 times in the afternoon and 9 times at night!

Morning

1.
2.
3.

Afternoon

1.
2.
3.
4.
5.
6.

Night

1.
2.
3.
4.
5.
6.
7.
8.
9.

DAY 1 2 3 4 5 6 7 8 9 10 11 12 13 14 15 16 17 18
19 20 21 22 23 24 25 26 27 28 29 30 31 32 33

Bye Money Blocks

What are your money blocks, or negative thoughts and outlooks you have about yourself or money?
i.e. Money is hard to come by, you'll never be able to pay off all your debt, etc. Instead, approach money
with an abundance mindset and reframe your thinking into a positive statement.

MONEY BLOCK	POSITIVE RE-WRITE
MONEY BLOCK	POSITIVE RE-WRITE
MONEY BLOCK	POSITIVE RE-WRITE
MONEY BLOCK	POSITIVE RE-WRITE

Nix the Negative

Ditch the negative self-talk and limiting beliefs by making it a regular habit to change those thoughts into positive ones! Putting yourself down will also bring down your energy so be your biggest cheerleader!

I CAN'T	I CAN
I AM NOT	I AM
I WON'T	I WILL
I DON'T	I DO

Checks from the Universe

Write out a check to yourself for the amount you wish to manifest. Imagine what you will feel like when the money hits your bank account!

THE UNIVERSE BANK

DATE ___________

PAY TO ___________ $ ___

MEMO ___________   SIGNATURE **The Universe**

THE UNIVERSE BANK

DATE ___________

PAY TO ___________ $ ___

MEMO ___________   SIGNATURE **The Universe**

THE UNIVERSE BANK

DATE ___________

PAY TO ___________ $ ___

MEMO ___________   SIGNATURE **The Universe**

Abundance Tracker

Sometimes we don't realize just how abundant we are! Write down every time you earn, find, or are gifted money. Being aware of your income helps you to be more grateful for all the money that comes into your life. Having a positive attitude towards money will allow you to attract more of it!

Month	JAN	FEB	MAR	APR	MAY	JUN	JUL	AUG	SEP	OCT	NOV	DEC

DATE	AMOUNT	SOURCE
Total		

Dreams Come True

Keep track of all your manifestations that become a reality each month!

January	February	March

April	May	June

July	August	September

October	November	December

Your Dream Life

You wake up one morning and realize you have everything you
have ever wanted. You are completely content and life is a dream!
What does your life look like?

Job

Yearly Income

Hobbies

Car

Relationships

Home

Money Mindset

It is important to have a positive relationship with money to attract more of it into your life. When you put out negative or desperate energy into the universe, you repel the very thing you want to attract. Think of money as something abundant and be grateful for what the money you have now has provided you. Use the chart below to write down all the positive things and emotions money has brought you in the past and will bring you in the future! Start being friends with money and more will come to you.

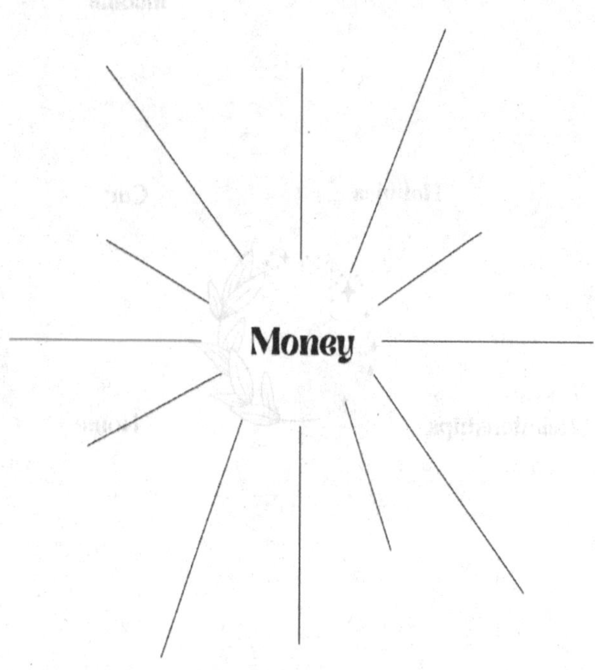

Vision Board

Bucket List

Write down everything you want to do , every place you want to go and everything you want to purchase when you are financially stable and living your best life!

Notes